WE STAY IN OUR OWN TREE

SHATTERING THE TABOO OF ABUSIVE INCEST

MICHELLE BARRY

CONTENTS

Editor: Sonny Marion Ock

Cover Design and Interior Design: Homestead Publishing Co. LLC.

Trigger Warning

This book has explicit language and sex scenes.

Dedication

To all survivors; you matter!

PREFACE

People squirm when they hear the word *incest*. One of my primary motivations in writing my memoir was to strip away the taboo associated with incest. At one time it was hard for me to say the word. But the more you say the word incest, the more it loses its powerful grip over you. If you can start by saying it to yourself, first, you've taken the first step.

Thankfully, the discussion around sexual abuse has evolved over time. Dialogue about incest, however, has a long way to go. If we can talk about it, we can address it and support those survivors, who like me, have lived through its horrors. The taboo continues to hold its power because the shame incest survivors experience can leave lifelong scars of self-loathing, bottomless guilt, depression, divided loyalties, and worst of all, secrecy.

Keeping secrets between family members inevitably rots family relations. Survivors need to help other survivors lift the shroud of secrecy which often keeps accounts of incest under lock and key, silencing victims while letting their abusers go free.

My journey of recovery has been a long one. Insomnia was one of my worst symptoms after I started recalling my abuse. While my body felt so tired, my mind was constantly racing on a never-ending treadmill of negative thoughts, obsessing over all the bad things that have happened and all the bad things that still might.

When I first began writing, it was a way to mediate my thoughts. After wrestling with my thoughts all night, I would get excited at the prospect of writing it all down, but when morning came so would all of my insecurities. How could I write all my experiences down when I couldn't yet put words to feelings that left me confused; I struggled with this emotional tug-of-war for years.

When I finally began writing regularly, I discovered how underreported stories like mine are because of pressures to keep up appearances within a family. In my search for answers to lifelong questions around identity, I discovered that I'm not alone in my struggles. Finally, there was a clinical lens through which I could understand the emotional aftershocks of my abuse, and I could see myself clearly for the first time.

If my story helps one person who is harboring this crippling secret to understand that she or he is not alone, maybe it will give that person the courage to speak out. Even if it risks fracturing family ties within your family tree. Countless times growing up, I was taught that *we stay in our own tree.* This was my dad's way of saying we mind our own business and we don't get involved in other people's either. For me, the cost of repossessing the lost parts of my identity required seismic shifts in my family tree. While learning the truth of my incestual abuse was painful, it was also the beginning of my recovery.

1

THE MONSTER

It doesn't matter where in the house I am. When he wants something from me, he finds me. The monster and I have been playing our secret touching games for a while now. Just seven years old, I'm sitting in the bathtub playing with the bubbles. I hear footsteps as the monster stops just outside the bathroom door, and see his shadow looming. He slides a note under the door; it's a sight I've come to dread.

The bath water goes from hot to cold in the time I struggle to decide what to do next. My heart is racing, as are my thoughts. If I do what he wants and get it over with, maybe he will be satisfied for a while. I feel nauseous with my stomach tied up in knots. Getting out of the tub and quickly toweling off, I refuse to look at my body because, even at this young age, I already tie feelings of shame to my body. Already knowing what it says, I flush his note down the toilet, getting rid of its evidence.

I open the bathroom door very quietly, so he doesn't hear me. Can I tip toe to my bedroom undetected? Reaching my bedroom safely, and after closing the door, I finally let out a sign of relief. I attempt to dress myself as quickly as possible, I want to get back downstairs where I'll be safe. After all, if I can reach my mom the monster won't come after me. Then I hear him on the move again, his footsteps quietly creeping until he's just outside my door. I know what's coming.

A second note appears under the door. It reads, *Come play a game, and choose your treasure.* The seemingly harmless words trigger me. My anxiety shoots through the roof and there's no way to calm the pressure I feel building up inside of me. I feel the heavy burden of the expectation to please him. By this point, I'm already well-groomed to satisfy the monster's needs and I've long abandoned the idea that my mom will come to my rescue. She rarely ventures into this part of the house. It's the monster's private domain.

With an overbearing sense of obligation, I walk across the hallway to his room. As I get closer, I can hear music by The Eagles blaring on the 8-track from inside the room. When the door opens, he puts his fingers to his lips warning me to be quiet as he beckons me inside. As the door closes, I step into his world. He is in control now and I know what I am expected to do.

Inside the room, the air is musty and pungent from the smell of weed. He keeps his room dark. The windows which would otherwise warm and brighten the room, are covered with bedsheets to block out the sunlight. The bare wooden floor is always cold underneath my feet. His black light posters of skulls and dragons taped to the walls keep me feeling uneasy. His room is littered with dishes and dirty clothes strewn everywhere. The bed's metal bedframe is always cold to the touch. There's a barren mattress atop a squeaky box spring. He never has sheets on his bed.

Carefully laid out on the bed are the trinkets he rewards me with for participating in his games. A necklace, a little wooden jewelry box, and a handwritten promise that I can listen to his 8-track for a full day. The necklace holds my interest but I know I'd have to hide it from my mom, so I point to the 8-track instead. However, I would gladly not take anything if it meant I didn't have to do what he wanted.

Quickly, the other bribes are cleared off the bed. After taking off every article of clothing he has on, he grabs a bottle of yellow lotion and lays down on the bed next to me. The room is cold and I notice the monster has goosebumps. After lubricating himself, he takes my hand and puts it on his penis. With his hand clasped over mine, he begins to stroke himself. This ritual is a familiar one.

After a while, he surprises me by saying, "I want you to put your mouth on my dick and give it kisses all over and then suck on it like a lollipop." It confuses me when the rules of the game change. Reluctantly, I put my mouth on his penis; it gives off a strong body odor of stale sweat. After kissing it for a while he tells me to put it in my mouth.

The penis is slippery and keeps popping out of my small mouth. After a few minutes of fumbling like this, I can sense his frustration. I have a strong desire to abandon what I'm doing. I want to jump off the bed and run out of the room despite knowing he will stay mad at me for the rest of the day. Still I say, "I don't want to do this anymore." He gives me an irritated look that I've seen before when I've protested.

"Keep trying," he insists and repositions himself on the bed so that the full shaft of his penis can slide in and out better. He is now fully erect. He puts his hand on my head and feeling the added pressure, I try not to gag. As he becomes more aroused, his breathing gets heavier, and he begins to thrust into my mouth faster.

I look for the signs that the icky stuff is going to come out. His eyes take on a hard, glassy, stare. When the white, milky, goop finally spurts forth, it goes all over the place. I am nauseated by the smell and try not to throw up.

As his breathing returns to normal, he sits up and takes a sock to wipe himself off, and then throws the soiled sock to me to do the same. He looks at me with a grin, and in a flash, the monster vanishes and the brother I love is back. I'm relieved the game is over. I know I've fulfilled my role in pleasing my brother. Having found no pleasure in this game whatsoever, I ask, "Can we go outside now and play a different game?"

"Yah, let's go built a fort. But remember don't tell nobody," he says, "If I get in trouble, you'll get in trouble too."

2

FAMILY TREE

My mom was born in the Smoky Mountains of Sevierville, Tennessee in 1936. Like my dad, she was born at home in a two-room house with no running water or electricity. Unlike my dad's folks, her family were poor hillbillies. My dad was a poor country boy. His family was poor but not like the hillbillies.

That area of Tennessee was as remote as remote could be. Isolation was a part of daily life, and my mom only had her parents and her siblings. Neighbors were not seen for months at a time. Their livelihood was through farming, fishing and hunting for bears, deer, wild turkey and small game. They drank well water and they lived off the land. Money was always in short supply, not only for them but everyone in that region, and bartering for staples was customary. It's how they got flour, sugar, and their coffee.

She said families back then had so many kids in order that there would be enough hands to work the farm. With so many siblings, fourteen of them, my mom could hardly hear her own voice. Even after she moved out and started her own family, she lacked the conviction to use the voice she had. She was predominantly a quiet and distant person. She never hollered or raised her voice. Rather than talking, she would listen, first to her husband, and then to her children. She was never one to vocally challenge you if she disagreed with you. She reconciled things in her own way.

While she was growing up, my mom lacked the parental affection that every parent should shower their children with. There simply was no time for hugs, kisses or bedtime stories. My mom remembers there was always more work to be done, and work always came first. It was a matter of survival. When my mom had her own kids, she was the same way. Because of the way her parents raised *her*, my mom rarely exhibited physical affection with any us. Of my siblings, I was the one exception, because I demanded it.

My Mom had a sister, Jesse, who was born in the 1920's. She contracted polio when she was just six years old. It was a time when parents would lock children with any type of disfigurement or abnormality in a room all day. Jesse was terribly isolated, while the rest of the family worked the homestead. She was not allowed to go to school, as it was frowned upon for kids who were in any way different to be seen in public. As a result, she grew up with developmental impairments and a lack of healthy social skills. At the onset of puberty, Jesse underwent a hysterectomy. With the mentality of a small girl, she had no say.

My mom considered herself fortunate in that she got to go to school and graduate. She went to grade school in the same two room schoolhouse as Dolly Parton. She went to college for about a year, where she met a city boy. They had a whirlwind courtship and got married. The marriage didn't last and was annulled. She remained close to a sister who'd moved farthest away from Tennessee. So at twenty-two years old, she traveled all the way to Montana to live with her sister, who was already a mom to four kids. It's in Montana that Mom and Dad met and fell in love.

My mom still blushes at the memory of how she met my

dad. He was the good-looking neighbor who lived across the street from her sister's house. Mom was starstruck by his good looks. So much so, that she began to look forward to seeing him when he returned home each night. She would sit in the window of her sister's home and start daydreaming about their future together. She had her sights set on meeting him and came up with the perfect plan.

Since she was eager to get his attention, she would mail blank letters in the mailbox beneath my dad's apartment window hoping he would notice her. Unbeknownst to my mom, he'd noticed her already as the pretty woman gazing out the window. Dad recalls Mom wearing an attractive pair of blue pants, which flattered her nice, full, figure. To this day, he still remembers that shade of blue.

He eventually asked her to go for a joyride with him. She said yes. Though he only took her around the block that first day, she fell madly in love and was ready to go around the world with him.

First came love, then came marriage, and then came Dylan, Caitlyn, Quint, Damien, and me. Dylan was born in in Butte, Montana. My dad went where the jobs were, and he was a good provider. Caitlyn, who was born a year later, was born in Gold Beach, Oregon. Then, exactly ten months later, Quint came into the world, in White Silver Springs, Montana where Mom and Dad chose to settle for four years. My mom always joked around that she wanted twelve hearty boys. She promptly changed her mind after giving birth to Quint, who was always her favorite. Caitlyn recalls this time in their marriage as the happiest of their lives. Five years later, Damien was born in Bear Creek, Wisconsin.

My dad was a rambler at heart, and my mom knew he could never be tied down in one spot for too long, even though he was the father of her five children. Instead of calling him Dad, my older siblings called him The Old Man. He often worked the most gruesome jobs just because they paid well. While he had the family pick up and move around a lot, he kept his children fairly isolated from the world in locations as far west as the mountains of Montana and the Grand Canyon. He worked very hard to provide for his family and it was a time in their marriage when my mom said, "Your Dad was very different then."

When my dad moved the family back to the mid-west to Bear Creek, Wisconsin, he returned to the region where he'd been ruthlessly abused in earlier years. His unspoken demons started to catch up with him. That's when he started drinking heavily, though it was mostly beer. Preferring to drink his pain away, he was always at the bar. In a town where everyone knew everyone, he had plenty of drinking buddies. Dad was born in Tigertown, a couple miles away from Bear Creek.

Sometimes I would forget that The Old Man was also once a little boy. By joining him on one of his many trips to Tigertown, I got to see the rundown two-room shack where he spent his childhood, in a home with no electricity or running water. It was hard for me to imagine anyone living this way.

He pointed out a lone tree in the front yard which was no taller than he was as a young boy, but which now towered above him. Mischievous and curious, he always needed to know what was down the road. In fact, though it often kept him away from family sometimes for months at a time, he was the most well-traveled person I knew. As I took a picture of my dad next to the lone tree, it dawned on me it was a living symbol of the isolation my father grew up with.

Returning to his childhood home brought back a rush of memories for my dad. While he's usually a man of few words, he opened up about his mother Violet O'Brien for the first time. One of his fondest memories was snuggling under the bedsheets between his parents, feeling warm and safe. When his mother became pregnant with her second child, she asked her firstborn, my dad, if he would like to name the baby, to which my dad said, "What about Connor?"

When my dad was just a young boy of four, he was awoken one morning hearing his mother's moans. He rushed out of bed and ran into the kitchen where he saw his mother hemorrhaging, laying helpless on the kitchen table, while giving birth. There was blood everywhere. He remembers trying to reach her, but someone grabbed him by the collar and removed him from the room so he wouldn't be further traumatized by the horror of what he saw.

The doctor who was present asked Violet to make a choice, her life or the life of her baby. She chose the life of her baby, Connor. She was only twenty-five when she died. Her surviving child grew up in town and was raised by his maternal grandparents. Over the years, The Old Man would tease his younger brother about getting the good life. Though he rarely spoke about his inner feelings, he confided that seeing his own mother die so horribly affected him his whole life.

My grandpa went courting soon after and married a woman named Vivian, who brought with her some very dark demons. She and my grandfather had five children, who she would abuse sexually. There was also rampant physical abuse. A victim of sexual abuse herself, she became the abuser when she threatened and victimized her biological children as well as my dad, who was her stepson, into incestual relationships with her and each other. This cycle of abuse went on until my dad struck out on his own, at the tender age of twelve. He found work on farms and often stayed in their barns, which put a roof over his head when he had no other place to call home. He never learned to read and write, something that always bothered him, as it limited his employment opportunities throughout his life.

As a young boy who'd left home before he was even a teenager, he continued to move from place to place. Surviving on any job he could get, he caught frogs for thirty-five cents a pound and picked vegetables as a migrant farmer. At the age of seventeen, he came back to visit his father. He always had a warm relationship with his dad, but Vivian went straight to work laying a trap for him. She called the police alleging that he raped her daughter June, when in fact, Vivian was the one putting pressure on my Dad to have sex with her and her daughter. The police believed Vivian's side of the story, and he went to prison for a year. After Dad got out of prison, he signed up for the army and went overseas. It was a time in his life he would never talk about. He answered us with, "It was what it was." Even though he often refused to talk about it, I knew the struggles of his early life changed him forever.

3

LIFE ON THE FARM

My parents eventually settled in an area of Michigan called Donken, where I was born and raised. The family moved to Donken to help my paternal grandfather with his farm when his health began to fail. Unfortunately, this would bring my father into close proximity with his abusive stepmother Vivian again, who would stay a fixture in our lives for the next several years. I grew up hating her because on some gut level I knew she changed my Dad for the worse. I would call her the Devil behind her back.

Donken is in the Keweenaw Upper Peninsula, the UP, as it's called. Donken got its start by being a railroad station in the 1800's for the lumber company which provided all the jobs there. As young kids, my best friends and I used to play on the tracks. My Dad's father, Oliver, used to burn wood chips in big furnaces for work. There was a general store and a post office in town. During prohibition everyone knew to buy their alcohol at a spot in town called the Blind Pig. With so many working men in the area, when jobs at the lumbar mill were plentiful, there was also a red-light district.

Houses built when the town was booming would later be abandoned.

Many years later, Donken would linger on the edge of death, with only a few families to keep it from becoming a ghost town. Grandpa Oliver had built a forty-acre farm at the end of the main road in Donken, and had no intention of leaving. He built it all of brick himself and painted it yellow. It was a large, square, house with a full basement and bath, steps leading up to a big kitchen, and a back door. On the same floor was the main entrance, a huge living room, adjacent to which was the master bedroom. From that floor was a long stairwell, which led to four bedrooms and a full bathroom upstairs. They raised pigs, chickens, and had lots of old barns on the land.

Having to see his stepmother Vivian everyday brought Dad's demons back in full force. According to my paternal aunts, he never told his father about the violations. The secret kept him forever in bondage. It was common knowledge Vivian always hated my dad. She was a jealous and vindictive person by nature, and she expressed no remorse in the years after my dad escaped her clutches. Because his pain stayed buried, as an adult he was never able to confront her about the abuse she inflicted, and his drinking spiraled out of control.

The first time I saw my dad crying was at my grandpa's funeral. It frightened me to see him so fragile and vulnerable. Later my dad described his father, whom he loved dearly as, "A gentle man with a big heart," and Dad grieved the loss of his father for years afterward.

In the first few years, my dad worked in the mines. With the collapse of the copper mines and the depletion of timber, there wasn't much work in the area. He would get contracts to tear down old buildings. He would also work in the woods clearing trees, a job all of his children learned to do alongside him. Even so, none of the jobs Dad worked for cash brought in nearly enough to support a family. Mom and the kids went on welfare. While it was common in those parts, having to accept welfare hurt his pride.

When the work dried up completely during the economic downturn, my dad started drinking brandy heavily along with his beer. The hard liquor brought out an abusive streak, and it was a bad time in their marriage. Out of sheer frustration, he started to get physical with Mom for the first time. Caitlyn recalls hearing our mother's cries behind their closed bedroom door. At the bars, he often got into fights and was kicked out from most every bar in Donken during this regretful period in his life. Losing his job and being unable to roam as he would've liked brought out the worst in him.

My usually passive and quiet mother refused to put up with this physical violence from her husband. She would threaten to leave our dad a couple of times on the occasions that he would physically intimidate her, and she actually did. She packed all four kids into the van, and would drive all the way to Tennessee to stay with her sisters. Our dad would always sweet talk her into coming back. Her belief that they were meant to be together always helped them to reconcile.

Life on the farm was very isolating. My mom, who was already very asocial, would only venture into town once a week for groceries. None of my siblings had any friends until they started high school. It's only then, that they started branching out. Mom and Dad did nothing to encourage our friendships; Dad always insisted we stay in our own tree.

Tired of accepting menial cash jobs in Donken here and there, and unable to be pinned down in one place for too long, Dad decided to go back on the road to find better-paying jobs. He would return to the farm, Mom, and us kids every couple of months, though it was customary that he'd back on the road again in no time. It's on one of these return visits, that I was conceived.

Sometimes his visits were as short as a week, but my mom always looked forward to her man returning and it seemed to rouse her from her normally sedentary life. Often, the house would fall into a state of disarray without Dad around. When we knew Dad was returning home, Mom would rouse all the kids in a collective effort to make sure the house was spotless before his return.

After my dad would leave, Mom would habitually fall into an emotional slump, becoming overly somber. While she didn't intentionally neglect her children, she was inattentive. Whenever my mom retreated into a state of quiet desolation, Caitlyn often stepped in to do all the chores that would otherwise go undone. She was also, in large part, responsible for maintaining the farm, by tending to the massive garden plots which were a primary food source for us. Caitlyn, who took the initiative to change my diapers and bathe me, would become a surrogate mother to me when our mom seemed to fade.

Dylan and Quint would be responsible for cutting wood and stockpiling it in our enormous woodshed until it was seasoned enough to burn. Wood was our primary source of fuel and we cut all our own wood; the farm's big wood stove was also how we heated our water. Growing our own food and cutting more wood were necessary chores that were never-ending.

Money was also scarce. Growing up, everyone always had a job to help support the family. One job Caitlyn was tasked with was selling vegetables in the local bars. It was a job she disliked, and she hated being spotted by her schoolmates who she always perceived as better off. We also regularly got our clothes second-hand from Goodwill; she still recalls the deep embarrassment she felt when a classmate came up to her saying, "That shirt used to be mine." Dad, who was the grandchild of immigrants, was stern and imposed a strong work ethic in Caitlyn as well as in my older brothers Dylan and Quint. He would often say, "You will do what you need to help this family."

Mom left the farm on a regular basis to go meet Dad wherever he happened to be working at the time. They would camp out and spend time together; she always looked forward to their time together as a couple and would return home happy. Mom put my older siblings, who were now in high school, in charge to keep an eye on Damien, Aunt Jesse, and me. Aunt Jesse had come to live with us permanently. We all had a hand in helping her.

Quint was larger than life. He had a very protective nature, and watched out for Mom. He was old-fashioned and often took matters into his own hands. Like my Dad, they both believed we stay in our own tree. Because father and son were so similar, they often butted heads.

Caitlyn, who like me, often felt the isolation of growing up on a big farm, attended the same schoolhouse that I would later attend through eighth grade. It wasn't until the start of high school when she really began to enjoy having a social life. Caitlyn had the newfound freedom to indulge her wild side. It's during high school that she would meet Patty, her best friend, who would one day become our future sister-in-law and Dylan's wife.

Dylan and Patty started dating almost as soon as they met. When Patty started high school at the age of fourteen, she readily joined Dylan and my other siblings in their shenanigans and everyone accepted and loved her as family even before she and Dylan legally tied the knot. Dating an O'Brien meant embracing all of the wild abandon that we were famously known for.

With all of my older siblings close in age; they were as close as siblings could be. Caitlyn would always end up tagging alongside the boys as they created mischief day in and day out. Quint, in particular, had a boundless curiosity and always needed to know what was beyond his reach.

The isolation of our forty acre farm was the perfect place for Dylan, Caitlyn, and Quint to have huge wild parties which would often go from noon to night. As Dylan and Quint headed into their rebellious teenage years, there are plenty of accounts of my older brothers finding trouble. My mom didn't have a disciplinary bone in her body, and while Dylan and Quint were often bailed out by my mom, it was my dad who was the disciplinarian. With him away from the house so much though, punishments from him were sporadic. Dylan and Quint loved racing their souped up cars on the backroads, and often had fun outracing the police, who normally patrolled the highways, by escaping down the dirt roads my brothers knew so well.

When Dylan was behind the wheel outrunning the cops, as he usually did, through the streets of town it soon became a wicked game of cat and mouse. The dangerous chase ended in Dylan's car flipping over, igniting on impact. While Dylan and Patty walked away with their lives, the accident resulted in two fatalities. As a consequence, Dylan went to prison for a year.

My mom, who was normally a quiet communicator, showed her fierce loyalty to her first-born son. She instructed Patty on the importance of always standing by your man. With Dylan suddenly under so much scrutiny, after the accident made headline news, Patty had to make the first adult decision of her young life. Courageously, she took my mother's words to heart and never left Dylan; they have been married fifty years now.

Dylan was so shaken by the experience that he never raced cars again. He went into prison as a boy and came out a man. He never forgave himself for the lives that were lost; he was a changed man who was riddled with a titanic sense of guilt.

It seemed as if my eldest three siblings were inseparable, a bond that didn't necessarily extend to Damien and me because we were five and ten years younger than the others. In fact, Damien was often left to his own devices. He never got the attention of his older siblings who might have helped him develop better social skills and critical developmental milestones like understanding personal boundaries. This limited his ability to exhibit empathy for those around him. With our dad physically absent so much of the time, and our mom emotionally unavailable though she was physically present, it meant Damien wasn't getting his emotional needs met from anyone. There was a void, and it was only a matter of time before a stranger, whom my dad blindly welcomed into our lives, would poison our family tree by claiming Damien as his own.

4

AN OLD FAMILY FRIEND

My Dad was fond of telling us all the time, "You should always help someone with less means than you." Over the years, this would mean Dad would bring many men home to the farm to work odd jobs. They were hitchhikers, wayward travelers, and guys down on their luck. My Dad, who was on his own since the age of twelve, knew what it was to go without. In part, his altruism fed his ego. He seemed to relish expressing his dominance over these men, who were now in debt to him. Unfortunately, he developed a blind side in that he was never wary of strangers, when he should have been. It never dawned on him that he would be opening the door to a predator who would then victimize his most vulnerable son. Damien would be forever changed.

Glen's arrival brought with it irreparable harm to our family. Dad introduced him as an old friend from his childhood. Glen took up residence at the farm the next three years, helping my dad build a house for my paternal grandparents on our land. He was paid with food, beer, and a place to stay.

My parents were foolhardy to be so trusting that they'd

leave my brothers and sisters alone with no one but Glen to supervise for days at a time. He was not only an inept babysitter, he was also opportunistic and had ideas of his own.

Soon after his arrival, Glen attempted to molest Caitlyn and a cousin of ours. Caitlyn recalls physically pushing him off of her and fleeing to safety. Being the most assertive and outspoken child, Caitlyn wouldn't be silenced and was the first to warn my parents about Glen's predatory habits.

My Dad talked to Glen once, and after getting another man's account of what happened, he minimized what Caitlyn told him and chalked it all up to a drunken evening in which Glen went too far. This enabled my mom to stand by my dad's poor judgment and she simply advised Caitlyn, who was ten at the time, to stay away from him. No one even considered that Glen would go on to abuse Damien, who was only five years old.

Caitlyn was the first to notice that Damien was Glen's shadow; Damien was so in need of a consistent father figure. Dad often took his older sons, and Caitlyn, to work with him on jobs that would put food on the table, but Damien, being a little too young, was always left behind. Damien must have felt lonely without a father's attention but our dad was simply too preoccupied. Glen, however, was there to step in.

Damien was easy prey for Glen because no five year old would have prior knowledge of what sex was, and therefore had no context for what qualified as sexual abuse. Damien may have also felt defenseless in the face of seeing Glen go unpunished after his attempt to abuse Caitlyn. Glen would continue to abuse Damien until the age of eight. Glen most likely groomed Damien in much the same way that Damien groomed me.

Without adult guidance, Damien never learned about boundaries, the link between action and consequence, or the difference between right and wrong. There was no healthy parental discipline during his formative years.

The few times Dad *was* around, Damien quickly learned to fly below his radar. He was eager to avoid our dad who was known to have a volatile temper. Damien feared Dad's uncontrolled wrath. Damien also never had the opportunity to exercise his social skills. He developed no close friendships with others who might have helped him develop empathy, compassion, respect, and trust. He was emotionally stunted.

5

LET'S PLAY A GAME

The Saturday it all starts is a typical day of watching morning cartoons with Damien. The rest of our morning is spent outside playing marbles and looking for snakes, of which we are unafraid, underneath all the lumber piles from the many demolition jobs of the old abandoned buildings on our farm. By this time, all of our older siblings have left the nest to start their adult lives. Damien, who is five years older, and I remain on the farm and spend countless hours together finding ways to amuse ourselves.

After playing outside to my heart's content, I go up to my room in the early afternoon and take out my coloring books. I have gotten very good at learning how to occupy myself, as I have no playmates my own age.

My brother casually saunters into the room, and after closing the door, sits on the corner of my bedspread. I get up from the floor, setting my coloring aside. I am thrilled to be getting special attention from him today.

Wearing a boyish grin, my ten-year old brother says to me, "Do you want to play a new game? It's a secret touching game."

Of course, I do! I am so excited.

And then, "You have to keep our game a secret; you can't tell anyone. This special secret is just between me and you."

"I can keep a secret," I say. I like being special, and I want to show my brother what a big girl I can be.

Next, he says, "Let me see you with your dress off. Take everything off."

I am confused by his words but I don't want him to leave so I take off my dress and panties and stand there naked before him. There is no shame in my nudity, as I am completely innocent and comfortable in my body.

With a small uptick of excitement I can detect in his voice, he directs me, "Come lay on the bed; this will be fun." Still, unsuspecting and open to anything, I go and lay down on my bed. I remember how the sun came in from the window warming my small naked body, as my brother lays down beside me.

With measured words he says, "I'm going to touch you down there between your legs, by your pussy." I hear a mix of anticipation and nervousness in his voice. I've never heard the word pussy before and wonder if he's learned it from other school boys while in the school yard. I know he's reading our older brother's dirty magazines which they've left behind, which are still hidden in the bathroom.

He puts his cold hands on my hoo-hoo; his touch is clumsy and heavy-handed.

This feels wrong.

So I tell him, "I don't want to play this touching game anymore."

Hearing my objection, he says dismissively, "If you don't want to play with me anymore, then you don't have to, but I won't play with you ever again."

He waits to see my reaction to his words. I panic because I want and need his attention. Seeing how effectively his threat plays out in his favor this first time, he threatens to deprive me of his affection in the future.

After a moment of tense silence, I tell him, "*Okay*, I'll continue playing with you."

Hearing what he interprets as consent, he opens my legs wider and looks at what's in between. Continuing with his fingers, he spreads the tiny folds of my lips apart. He moves his fingers in a circular fashion probing me.

"Doesn't this feel good?" He looks for a sign to continue touching me.

"It doesn't hurt. But it doesn't feel good either," I explain to him.

"Well," he's says defensively, "the more we do it, the better it will feel."

He put his hands down his pants, which stay buttoned, and starts to rub himself. When I ask what he was doing, he replies, "I'm touching myself the way I'm touching you right now."

"I think Mom will get mad at us for playing this game."

"Then don't tell her," he replied. "It'll be our little secret."

He gets a sly look in his eyes that I haven't seen before; for the first time, I see the face of a monster who I was sure always lived under my bed. The perception of my brother as a monster only grows as I continue to be abused by him on a regular basis, over the next eight years.

BETRAYAL BLINDNESS

Before the abuse starts, I am just learning how to
trust and who to trust. On countless afternoons,
while seated on my mom's lap in our living room, I
find her maternal touch comforting to me. As a reserved
woman, she rarely says a word or expresses her emotions
outwards, but I always feel safe in her bosom. She has a way
of caressing my forehead that makes me feel loved.

As my mom's youngest, she picks me up and envelops
me in her large arms when I run to her. My older siblings
later tease that I am spoiled rotten, being able to crawl into
Mom's lap whenever I've wanted. They never received the
physical affection I did. I am the exception.

Despite being physically close to my mom, I am missing
the emotional interaction I desperately need but am not
getting from her. Though I sat in her lap, she often seems too
lost in her own thoughts. My mother never reads me books
and never plays games that might otherwise engage me. For
this sort of attention, I always turn to my brother Damien to
fill my emotional needs.

Damien is someone I love and trust. I can always trust

family; this is what I've always heard from my parents. It's the O'Brien way. We do everything together and we're always there for each other. Always.

At this age, I have no gage for what is appropriate or inappropriate. Up until this point, sex has no place in my world. It's an age when I am still learning right from wrong, and my brain is still developing such distinctions. The abuse also blurs my role in the family as well as my role in relation to my brother. Instead of the carefree child I have always been, I begin to wrestle with darker feelings that I don't understand. [1]

He effectively grooms me for increasing stages of sexual engagement as what happens between us rapidly progresses. The developmental stages which would normally take place in establishing a strong foundation of identity is repeatedly interrupted by my trauma. I never learn the core of who I am. [2]

He uses my love for him against me; it's the primary way in which he successfully gains leverage over me time and time again which enables him to thoroughly brainwash me. My incestual experiences with my older brother from the ages of six through fourteen result in my betrayal blindness, an adaptive way for my brain to process and then bury what I was experiencing. [3]

I later learn my reaction in coping this way is nonpathological, meaning that every healthy child would also react this way under similar abusive conditions. At an age when my brain should primarily be assigned to learning tasks, a stage of development which neurologists call the learning brain, I instead shift rapidly into functioning at the level of brain stem called the survival brain. [4]

As my turmoil continues into my teenage years, I drink excessively and struggle with my body image. Because I am forced to be a little adult who engages in adult acts from a

young age, I adapt to living as one and mature well beyond
my young years.[5]

Damien robbed me of my childhood.

THE THREE MUSKETEERS

I was seven years old when I met my two best friends, Roger, and his sister Wendy Lou. At this point the abuse had been going on for a year. We were a trio, and nothing could separate us; I spent as much time with them as possible. Wendy Lou is still my best friend to this day. She and I have experienced more loss than we could ever have been expected to bear, and through all the highs and lows we have been there for each other.

My mom gave me free-rein, and with our houses only a half mile apart, we would meet halfway and spend our days together. We would do everything: run through the woods and make forts with the sticks and leaves, we'd go into all the old abandoned buildings and occupy ourselves playing house and office for hours at a time. Roger and I would role-play in these early years; he was the dad, and I was the mom. It was a glimpse into our future feelings for each other.

Roger and Wendy Lou's Dad owned a construction company. Krause Construction was a successful business and the Krause name carried weight in the community. One of Roger's favorite things to do was to work on old cars.

We'd get 'em running, and after siphoning gas out of his Dad's work vehicles, Roger would get behind the wheel and we'd joyride for miles on long, winding, logging roads until the car Roger had fixed broke down and stopped working. Then we did it again. We knew every inch of Donken. It was our playground.

Dad hated the commercialism of a holiday like Christmas. So much so, that there were no presents, no trees, no lights, nothing. All I wanted at that age was a Barbie Dream House. There were few things I was jealous of, but Wendy Lou having a Barbie Dream House finally gave us something to fight about. After a couple of Christmases with no presents, my mom somehow found the money to get me a record player that was in a blue box with a latch, and some roller skates. While I knew I would have to hide the record player and skates from my dad, I was the happiest eleven-year-old in the world. Music became a way for me to escape and I relied on music more and more, in order to cope, after Damien started playing his games with me.

I buried my conflicted feelings not knowing how to deal with the turmoil. Damien's emotional attachment to me became more evident as I spent more time with Wendy Lou and Roger. He seemed threatened by my friendship with them, and resented any time I spent with them. He would also turn up uninvited when I was with my playmates. They thought it was weird that he seemed so possessive of me. They would make comments at the frequency of his appearances, and his seeming need to check up on me, but they never questioned the true nature of my relationship to my older brother.

Once a month, I hopped on a school bus and made the forty-mile trip to the nearest big town, a place called Houghton. There was no library in the two-room schoolhouse all my siblings and I attended. Seeing the rows and rows of records in the Houghton library, my eyes got big. I'd carry out a huge stack of records every time I left there. My all-time favorite was Neil Diamond; his music was a great escape. In fact, his songs saved my life throughout the many low points of my life. When I finally got to see him in concert, I cried the whole time.

During our long Michigan winters, my mom and I baked cakes and spent the afternoons playing Rummy with a deck of cards at the kitchen table. My mom would allow me a cup of her instant coffee, and we'd play music. Hours would pass and music would fill the walls of our home: legendary crooners like Johnny Cash, Kenny Rogers, Loretta Lynn, Dolly Parton, and Tonya Tucker would sing the soundtrack of our lives.

8

THE TREE FORT

When I was nine years old, Damien took my virginity. We went to the fort that I'd helped him build; it was a place where we'd idled away countless hours playing my favorite childhood game of Cowboys and Indians. It was a familiar place, where I'd often invite Wendy Lou and Roger to climb the surrounding maple trees and explore the beauty of the woods. The fort, at the edge of the farm, was fairly secluded because it was in the woods. It was the perfect secret hideout, and until that day, I'd made some very good memories there.

Damien kept all his cigarettes and dirty magazines hidden in a wooden box that he'd built. He was always good at making things with his hands. By this point, we were well past the grooming stage in which I was engaged in games he disguised as child's play.

Walking along a trail on our way to the fort, he said, "Do you want to look at some dirty magazines?" The nude pictures of centerfolds depicted women who had soft curves and the pronounced breasts that come with maturity. He asked, "Don't you want to be like them?" My thoughts centered on my nine-year old body, and how I looked nothing like the women in the pictures.

Attempting to prime me for what he was envisioning next, he went on to say, "Men put their dicks in their pussies. We can be like a couple. That's what people in love do." I began to understand his intention that his penis would be inside of me. A part of my pleasing behaviors was still wanting to see my big brother happy. But I was hesitant and asked, "Does it hurt?" He minimized the significance of what was about to take place.

He said, "It will be like a mosquito bite, and I will stop if it hurts too badly." In hindsight, knowing that he also lost his virginity to me that day, as I'm certain I was the only girl he had ever been with since Glen abused him, perhaps he had no true reference for how much physical pain it ended up causing me.

We both took off our clothes and laid down on an old blanket he had taken from the house weeks ago. It now smelled like the wet leaves. The air cooled my skin but I recall it was still warm enough to be nude outside. It was almost the end of summer.

He took out the Vaseline lotion that he had always used as a lubricant for our genitals. His penis was fully erect when he proceeded to lay on top of me. I recall his bodyweight being so heavy, I felt smothered. With the differences in the size of our bodies, he fumbled around trying to find the small opening of my vagina. When he penetrated me, his initial thrust caused a sharp pain that ripped through my whole body and I felt as if it would rip me in two. I immediately cried out and tried to push him off of me, begging for him to stop, but breaking his promise, he wouldn't. He looked nothing like my brother; his eyes were black, and I knew I was being consumed by the monster. I felt helpless.

He kept saying, *"I'm sorry, I'm sorry, but I can't stop."* In that moment, I understood he was choosing his own pleasure over my pain. His self-seeking gratification, which was evident in this moment, was characteristic of the man he would become.

The pain was so physically nauseating, that I thought I had passed out. I remember leaving my body and in my dissociated state I was suddenly cast into a far corner of the fort watching him on top of a little girl I recognized as me. She has her head turned sideways, with her eyes closed and her fists clenched. No one was there to stop him.

Not wanting to be a witness any further to the monster ravaging the little girl, I looked away from them both and fixated on the leaves of gently swaying trees above me, with the bright blue sky beyond. I heard the birdsong of the chickadees and saw squirrels scurrying along tree branches leaping from tree to tree. In actuality, there was a roof sheltering us in the enclosed space of the fort.

Sensing Damien's bodyweight lift off of me after he was done, I felt myself returning to my body, as if drawn back into my physical form by a psychic cord that my dissociated self was tied to. When I finally looked at him, he was crying and was trying to get the words out that he was sorry he hurt me. I could only stare at him; I was relieved to see the monster was gone. With my brother back, I tried to calm myself.

As I sat up, he was the first to notice the blood as a result of my deflowering and he quickly gathered some leaves to put between my legs. Looking down at myself, the red streaks that had trickled down between my legs were now drying as crimson stains. There was more blood I found in the fibers of the wool blanket, which he would later burn. The injury caused by the penetration left me terribly sore and I would be in a state of physical discomfort for a long time afterwards.

When he asked if I was okay, I didn't pretend that I was.

"What if I bleed to death?" The penetration had felt like he had cut me with a knife. Suddenly shaky at the sight of my own blood, I whimpered, "I want Mom, I want Mom."

"You're gonna be okay. You don't need to go see Mom. If you do, she'll want to know why you're bleeding down there. We'll both get in trouble."

"I don't want to do that again."

Shamelessly, he said, "I couldn't help myself; guys can't stop once they start."

With those few words, he justified for himself what he just did. Perhaps the act of losing our virginity to each other was also an act of consummation, similar to what might happen emotionally between a man and his wife. The sexual act itself nurtured the emotional attachment between us, binding us in such a way that made it impossible for me to betray someone I was already so deeply attached to. His secret was safe with me.

9

SOMEONE NOT ME

Thereafter, Damien's sexual appetite became more voracious, and he began begging. I didn't feel special anymore, and the attention I was getting from him now put unwanted pressure on me. I felt obligated to surrender my body to him, in order to keep him happy. He'd conditioned me from the very start to cater to his happiness. Reflecting on that time in my life now, those times when he was begging me for sexual favors, and somehow always getting his way with me, I realize what an effective job he'd done of brainwashing me.

His favorite position was missionary position, and as he was gratifying himself I would go far, far, away. Looking down on what was happening, and numb to any and all physical sensation, I began to make the mental leap, just as I did on the day I lost my virginity, that the girl underneath Damien, plastered under his heavy bodyweight, was someone else. Someone not me. Before the abuse ended, Damien and I were having sex up to four or five times a week.

By the time Damien was sixteen, and I was eleven, Damien was now old enough to watch Aunt Jesse and I, and

Mom left him in charge when she would leave to go meet my dad. I was used to helping out around the house, cooking all the meals and regularly helping Aunt Jesse with everything from bathing to combing her hair.

As a teenager who was practicing sex, it was only a matter of time before he also began to exploit our disabled Aunt Jesse, to feed his sexual appetite. Having already taken my virginity two years before, he was now looking to experiment. Causing me much shame in retrospect, Damien would regularly ask me to convince Aunt Jesse to drink a beer or smoke a cigarette. He would then threaten and bargain with her, sometimes cruelly taking away her television soaps, which were her only real source of enjoyment. Though she only had the mind of a six-year old she knew what sex was. She would eventually consent, and Aunt Jesse and Damien had a sexual relationship. I will never forgive myself for participating in this. I still have nightmares of scenes with Damien on top of Aunt Jesse.

When I was younger, before the abuse began, Damien had my complete trust, and therefore I was easily coerced by him. As my abuse was ongoing, I learned to distrust my own instincts which screamed out that what I was enduring at his hands was completely wrong. My silence, which was also ongoing, only added to a complicity which resulted in a deep sense of self-hatred for myself. I started to do anything to avoid Damien and sought refuge in my friendships with Roger and Wendy Lou.

The three of us continued to see each other everyday. My secret, however, remained entirely shrouded; I told no one. Most of all, I feared that if anyone found out, especially my best friends, then I would no longer be able to pretend that it wasn't happening.

I was nine and had just started fifth grade, but I no longer felt like a little girl anymore. I felt like I had to parade around in the *disguise* of a little girl, and felt worlds apart from other kids my age. It was very isolating. The things that preoccupied them suddenly seemed trivial to me; I felt like an ugly duckling and was socially awkward. Everyone else seemed normal to me. In contrast, I felt like anything but. I wondered if others could see the changes that had taken place in me.

Roger and Wendy Lou, who so easily befriended other kids, motivated me to act like someone else. Someone who wasn't chronically lonely, and someone who wasn't so self-conscious about the secret I harbored. I developed a youthful alter-ego who was wild and fun; I so wanted to be accepted as cool. When I started to get into trouble with my teachers and the principal of the school, I knew I was getting somewhere. It was a time when a smack on the knuckles with a ruler was still customary. Whether the attention I got was negative or positive, I enjoyed this newfound freedom. Attention from Roger, who I loved most of all, enabled me to keep him close and our future feelings for each other would soon intensify.

10

MY FIRST TRUE LOVE

Wendy Lou, Roger, and I were always together, the three musketeers. And I don't remember a time when I wasn't in love with Roger. Wendy Lou always seemed to know that Roger and I loved each other. He kissed me for the first time when I was nine and we started experimenting with sex when I was eleven and he was thirteen. By that time, with our hormones in full swing, we were always trying to ditch Wendy Lou so we could be alone together. She would throw a fit, always wanting to be included in everything we did. She was more understanding when she began realizing our young adult feelings for each other.

When Roger and I were together, I felt better about myself. He made me feel beautiful, normal even. In the safety of his arms, everything else disappeared. One warm summer night, just before he started high school, we were laying under the stars in his back yard. With our faces just inches away from each other, I had fears the start of high school would mean we'd soon be drifting apart.

"We're so used to being together every day, it's gonna be weird being apart from you for the first time," I said.

With our families being from two different social classes, Roger was destined to be popular. His family's standing in the community opened doors for him that weren't available to me. He was driving now, and his high school would be full of new kids hailing from the surrounding area. Seeing my concern, Roger looked me in the eyes and told me, "We will *never* be apart."

Slowly we started moving in different circles until I felt like we were inhabiting two different worlds. Even as we drifted apart, my love for him never changed. As we matured, we started to test the waters and dated other people. His friends always pulled him in a different direction. But no matter who else we were dating, we could never seem to let go of each other.

Almost every night we still found our way into each other's arms. My parents had no objections to sleeping over at Wendy Lou's, and she invited me often. Roger would always sneak into the room, while Wendy Lou slept, and after waking me up, he'd grab me by the hand and lead me to his bedroom. With his head on a pillow, I'd lay on his chest and he'd hold me while we talked. He'd cup his hand under my chin and lift my head up, until our eyes met. Then, he'd lean in and kiss me gently. Feeling a surge of new desire, his kisses would become more consuming, as his mouth traveled from my lips to my ears, where he'd then whisper, "I will always love you."

Gently tugging at my shirt, it was his way of asking me to take my shirt off. After I disrobed, I would do the same for him. We'd switch places on the bed, and with me laying on my back, he's cup my breasts, gently caressing and kissing them. My fingertips would gently run up and down his smooth, built, back as we found pleasure in each other. Nights like these were ours and ours alone. As longtime childhood friends, we knew the language of each other's bodies so well, that by this point, no words were needed. When we made love, I could hear his every sigh and I felt perfectly at peace. I felt like my heart would burst sometimes, I loved him so much. He was my sanctuary and my hope for the future; we made plans to be together.

11

DADDY'S LITTLE GIRL

W hen I was younger, I adored my Dad and thought he could do no wrong. I was his little girl. He was so handsome and charismatic. His charming smile always made me happy. Dad would always tell me he loved me. The word 'love' was always used in our house. As a result, when Damien used the word 'love' to get what he wanted, I was deeply confused.

Though my Dad was not in the house often, he was incredibly affectionate with me and I lacked for nothing. His favorite thing was to get home in the middle of the night in order to surprise me with his presence the next morning. As I wandered into the kitchen, he's scoop me up in his arms and I'd cry gleefully, *"Daddy!! You're home!"* His laughter was infectious. A rhyme he often sang to all of us kids growing up was, "I love you a bushel, and a peck, and a hug around the neck."

I'll always cherish his favorite term of endearment for me. He called me his *moonbaby*. As I grew up, he would retell the story for me countless times. As a newborn baby, I was swaddled and placed in a bassinet in my parent's bedroom.

The moonlight would shine down upon the bassinet, illuminating my tiny body. As I grew older, Dad was fond of telling me that I always pointed to the moon when it lit up the sky and said, "My moon." He said, "Daughter, you stopped on the moon before you came to be with me and your mom."

I remember the first time I saw my Dad's mean side with my own eyes. He made Damien and I sit on the couch. My Mom was in her chair, as usual. He made us an unwilling audience, and having our attention, he then threw Quint up against the wall. Damien and I were so scared, we held onto each other's hands. My Dad had a ferocious intensity in his eyes and his face was as hard as marble. In a rage, he didn't look handsome anymore. He had caught Quint smoking. As a punishment, my Dad would light a cigarette and make Quint smoke one after another. This seemed to go on forever. He'd slap Quint and say to him, "You want to be a man? You want to defy me? Be a man and smoke this whole pack." I looked over at my mom, and she had tears streaming down her face. Seeing how upset my mom was, my dad says defensively, "JoAnn, you know I have to do this."

My mom never said a word. Damien and I tried not to look at Quint. My dad hollered at us, "You'll watch your brother try and be a man." I hated seeing Quint like this; he was my hero. He was just standing there taking my dad's abuse with this hurt look in his eyes. All Quint ever wanted was my dad's approval. I was crying so hard that I jumped up and ran to Quint and put my arms around his legs. I screamed at my dad to please stop; he looked at me with those fierce eyes and then it was as if he woke up from something. Finally, his eyes softened and his face relaxed. He said, "You and your brother go to bed now." He looked at Quint and told him, "I don't ever want to see you smoking again, go to your room." I started not liking my dad so much after that, knowing that the man who I adored could be so cruel.

It's not long after that, that I found out from Patty that Dad was regularly unfaithful to Mom. When I defended Dad, she lashed out, "Your dad cheats on your mom all the time." I was completely crushed to hear those words. I'd always thought my mom and dad had an epic love for each other. They were soulmates, and said so often. To know that my dad was cheating shattered the ideal I had of my parents and I never looked at them the same way again.

I couldn't unknow what I now knew about his sexual indiscretions. I saw him through new eyes, and lost respect for him. I saw him through my sibling's eyes now. I finally understood why they hated the old man. Taking after my siblings, I began calling him The Old Man as well. I finally saw him for the drunk, cheating, mean asshole he was. He sensed my newly changed feelings. I was no longer his sweet little girl who adored him. As if to punish me, he became even more domineering.

12

GOODBYE, LAZY DAYS

My mom got sick with leukemia when I was just eleven years old. With my mom now ill, my older sister Caitlyn felt it imperative that my dad return to the farm and stay put. His wife needed him. Dad, with more time spent on the road than at home, fought this obligation to tend to his wife's needs. He didn't want to face the music. If he did, he'd also have to admit to himself that she was dying. They had an inexplicable bond. The doctors gave her a year, but always one to try all the latest cancer drugs, she fought hard and rallied for a number of years before we lost her.

We all had to make changes to accommodate my mom. A common cold could have been a death sentence, so we made sure the house was thoroughly disinfected and sterilized. My dad, who had always been a clean freak, took every precaution. House guests were stricken form the house; we didn't want to expose Mom to any germs that might sicken her. She began to waste away slowly. By the end of her life, she'd gone from three hundred pounds to half her body weight. The new drugs were making her terribly nauseous and weak, but I never once heard her complain.

With Dad now living at home, gone were my endless lazy days of playing with Wendy Lou and Roger. I got to know my father in a way that I hadn't before. All his shortcomings were on display on a daily basis. His flaws included a sharp temper and a mean streak. Damien was in Wisconsin, and with all of my other siblings also out of the house, I was the only one who remained. Now that my dad's traveling days were over, he was drinking more. In order to support his habit, he started selling wood for money and I was enlisted to help.

My life during that period was an endless parade of chores and obligations in which all my days started blending together. My dad required me to do the same backbreaking woodwork day in day out and was as demanding as a slave driver. My days started at 5am with chores before I would board the school bus. After school, upon immediately coming home I, again, had to dedicate all of my available time to hauling, piling, lifting, splitting, and delivering cords of wood. Whenever we'd take a rest, my dad would shout out, "Beer Break!" and he'd crack open a Pabst Blue Ribbon, tossing another one to me. The manual labor didn't seem as hard when I was buzzed. I was permitted a half hour break for dinner and worked continuously until dark.

In addition to working for my dad, I picked up babysitting jobs anytime I could. It was a welcome change from the backbreaking work of hauling wood. Juggling both jobs, my schedule never changed, and between the ages of twelve to sixteen I felt exiled in the woods while everyone else was growing up around me.

As Roger became more popular, it killed me that I wasn't seeing him as often. I feared our different lifestyles were pulling us apart, and I put the blame squarely on my Dad's shoulders.

I squeezed in time to do homework in the late evening hours or while I was babysitting. The weekends were just as grueling, even more so. I would get up at five in the morning for a full day of chopping wood. I sacrificed any time I might otherwise dedicate to having a social life to helping my father support the family. With no life of my own, I grew bitter and resentful. I told myself that I would do better for myself one day.

I was allowed to babysit as much as I wanted, and was able to keep most of my babysitting money for myself. I made a dollar an hour. Babysitting since the age of nine years old, I eventually had enough saved to have an impressive nest egg. In my mind, babysitting was my way out from the farm. With The Old Man on the farm all the time now, his overbearing presence only made me want to escape sooner.

13

EARLY BLOOMER

My body blossomed at an early age and after I started my period, my body seemed to change overnight. Caitlyn bought me my first pair of jeans as a gift; I was officially a woman. My clothes from Goodwill had always made me feel self-conscious. I never felt pretty.

When Roger noticed how the jeans enhanced my new curves, he complimented me on how nice I looked. This made me feel wonderful. It helped me to look at my body with less shame. With the onset of puberty, I also lost the bodyfat around my face and belly. My breasts developed and I looked like a girl older than my true age. My womanly curves brought with it a lot of unwanted attention from older men.

When I was eleven and twelve years old, I spent two summers in Tennessee with my maternal aunts and my cousins. Spending time with my cousins David and Penny was an introduction to a whole new world that involved normalizing myself to reckless sexual behaviors, experimenting with drugs, and of course, loads of drinking.

It was your typical suburb in Kingston, TN, but to me I was dropped off in a whole new world. It was the first time I saw white picket fences, manicured lawns, and houses so close together that it brought neighbors closer.

Penny, who was around the same age, was very wild. To me, I saw her as more worldly than me. Penny was having sex with her brother also, and this shared experience incited her to show me how she started using sex as a means to get what she wanted. For cigarettes and booze, Penny and I would go to the old men's houses who were in the neighborhood and let them touch us.

The old men would put their wrinkly, hairy, hands down our pants and play with our vaginas. Their stale breath often reeked of booze and beer. I would close my eyes and wait for it all to be over. I remember thinking that this was no worse than what Damien had already done to me. The line between involuntary and voluntary participation was completely blurred. After one house we'd go to the next, sometimes two or three men's houses in a day. My vagina would be sore at the end of the day.

We would always go back home before dark to eat dinner and then pretend to go to bed. Then we'd sneak out and party all night. We did this all summer. We would take the booze and cigarettes we'd procured during the day to the older kid's houses and hang out to party with them. Drugs were plentiful. Penny, who was always more brazen, would have no qualms about approaching older guys who were eighteen and older asking, "Would you like to have sex with me?" I don't recall anyone ever refusing her.

High on drugs, we'd do wild and reckless things to win a bet; we'd take turns lying down on the painted double lines in the middle of a dark road at night. The headlights of the oncoming car were the only illumination. When the driver behind of wheel would swerve, the person who won the bet would walk away with her life. I spent those summers in a haze and even though I knew this was my new normal, I hated myself for participating. It would be years before I would remember the things I engaged in those lost summers in Tennessee. Sometimes now, when I smell something, be it a lit cigarette, a certain brand of booze, or the sap of a pine tree, I'm triggered and all those buried feelings of shame and self-hate resurface.

When I returned to Donken after my summers spent in Tennessee, I always resumed my friendships with Wendy Lou and Roger, which was a source of great comfort to me. They were my everything, and provided me with the only normalcy I ever knew. We were all alike in that we had older siblings. Dylan was eleven years older than me. Ron, who was Dylan's classmate, and Wendy's older brother, was older than Wendy Lou by twelve years. Once puberty hit, Ron, who'd never even acknowledged I'd existed, was suddenly paying attention and would try and cozy up to me as often as possible.

At first blush, I was flattered that he noticed me when he began to offer me rides to and from Wendy Lou's house. What first appeared as a kind act was really his way of getting me in the car alone. One day, before we ever reached the farm, he pulled off the main road and parked the car. I became very nervous because we were so secluded. I could see the way things were headed and if he wanted to do more than talk, I was in trouble. I felt like a deer caught in headlights.

He molested me that night and it added to my self-hatred because, after all my experiences in Tennessee, I let it happen, even though I felt utterly violated while it was happening. It was just one more secret that I was learning to repress that would in future years become a memory I would have no recollection of. The secrecy of what happened with Roger's brother was something I never wanted him to find out. Ron continued to show interest in me, but I learned to avoid him after I pushed what happened out of my mind. Wendy Lou and Roger never found out.

14

GAME OVER

Once in high school, Damien met Steve who befriended him and introduced him to pornography. It was much more explicit than the dirty magazines. Though high school was an opportunity for him to expand his horizons, Damien stayed largely solitary with Steve being his only friend. Damien's porn habit seemed to intensify his sex drive even more, sending him into overdrive. As my abuse continued, I saw a new brutality in my brother and saw him as a monster more and more. There were no more juvenile games, now our relationship was completely hard-core. He started using *all* the explicit phrases like, "suck my cock" and "fuck your cunt." Our sex was unemotional.[6]

Together, they were drinking and smoking pot, and getting into all sorts of trouble. My mom would always bail Damien out. One time they broke into someone's house and stole a bunch of stuff, destroying the house in the process. My mom couldn't help this time; it was out of her hands. Damien and Steve got six months each. After he finished his jail term, my dad sent Damien to Wisconsin to live with Dylan and Quint, to learn from their work ethic and to show Damien how to work a steady job.

I had two more years of high school, and I was living under a constant black cloud. Though I was physically in one piece, my sense of self was fragmented. I lived in a dissociative state. I was living my life from the outside looking in, and everything seemed unreal, dull, and dreary. I began to drink even more, and it was a great escape.

With Damien gone, I was on my own for the first time. I just started high school, so my social network was expanding. When I was drinking, I liked the way I felt because I didn't have to be me for a little while. The usually self-conscious, shy girl who didn't fit in at school was confident and full of personality. The personality change was so strikingly different from who I normally was, I felt like I embodied an alternate personality. By then it was so easy to switch back and forth, it came naturally to me. Much less uninhibited when drinking, I was suddenly funny, which attracted the attention I craved. Everyone couldn't believe how different I was from my persona in school. I made some new friends other than Wendy Lou and Roger, who were in turn meeting new people.

I started seeing the ways other people interacted with their families. For the first time, I observed how other girls communicated with their parents and with their siblings. I observed how differently my friends' parents addressed their kids; what was said and what went unsaid. Small everyday expressions such as, "How was your day," and "What did you do today," completely surprised me.

My family dynamics were polar opposites of the norm. It felt foreign to me how in my friends' families, their feelings were expressed and not hidden. Also, all their creature comforts, their fashionable clothes, their interest in hair and makeup, and their free time to lounge about their living room watching TV with tons of junk food at their disposal was a complete departure from everything I knew. I enjoyed my newfound independence and social life, free from Damien's emotional hold over me. I now had new friends to connect with emotionally and I was no longer solely dependent on Damien for my needs. The twisted cord between him and I was slowly disentangling.

My brother Damien was back home after a year away living in Wisconsin with my brothers. My mother was losing her battle with leukemia by this point, with a terminal diagnosis of six months to a year. I found myself feeling conflicted about my brother's return; after a year, I'd managed to detach myself from the years of sexual abuse.

One afternoon, Damien and I were sitting in his bedroom and he said, "Do want to play a game?" They were the same words I'd heard him say countless times before when I was a young child. Something in me just went cold and I knew I couldn't do it again. I told him, "We can't have this kind of relationship anymore."

Seeing the hurt look on his face, I feared how our relationship would change if I patently rejected him. I still valued the sibling connection, and I didn't want to threaten that bond. After every sex act, we'd never talked about what really transpired between us. Both of us always acted as if nothing had taken place.

He protested by saying, "But we love each other." I tried to get him to understand the difference between brotherly love and romantic love. Loving Roger, I never experienced one iota of shame and guilt. His love was liberating to me. In Roger's presence, I was able to let go of my worries and I felt truly safe in his arms. It came with none of the collateral damage, namely feelings of extreme shame and guilt, that always came with me submitting to Damien's version of love.

"But Roger doesn't love you like I do," Damien said defensively. Knowing I was truly in love with Roger, it begged the question, had my brother Damien really fallen for me? Could something that perverse actually have happened? I had kept my secret from Roger and Wendy Lou for a long time and I would continue to do so. Roger and the love we shared was simply too important to me; I would never jeopardize our relationship under any circumstances.

As if reading my mind, or seeing through me, Damien threatened me with, "What would Roger think if he knew about us?" I wore a poker face, though I was trembling inside. I looked him in the eye and told him, "I won't do this anymore and if you ask me to play this game ever again, I will tell everyone our secret." My words were an empty threat; I wasn't ready to swing an axe at our family tree. Knowing that I wasn't strong enough yet to expose him, I tried to speak as steadily as possible so he wouldn't call my bluff.

With a cold look in his eyes, I saw something dislodge in him. He felt the meaning behind my words. So I went on, "I don't ever want to talk about this again. I want to forget about this part of our history and we'll just be brother and sister again." He could tell by the tone of my voice that I was serious. He said, "You will never be able to forget."

Me standing up for myself that day, changed things for the better. Damien never asked me to play a game again. I took all my memories, put them in a far corner of my mind that I couldn't reach, and threw away the key. For others who share the same trauma, this is called betrayal blindness. The trauma goes underground and doesn't resurface until the day your mind is ready to face the agony. Until then, there's amnesia. There was no recollection in my mind of any of the abuse that had taken place. Though my mind had done a complete job of removing actual memories of my abuse, the feelings associated with the abuse were still there: feelings of worthlessness, shame, guilt, and utter self-hatred only grew stronger.

I didn't see too much of Damien over the next few years. Our lives were beginning to take us in different directions. With Damien's attention diverted from me, he soon met Helen and they started dating. Eventually, Damien and his girlfriend moved out west, where he and my brothers were on the oil rigs in Wyoming and the logging operations of South Dakota. With Damien gone and out of the house, I was able to start living as a halfway normal teenager. My feelings for Roger, my first true love, continued to deepen with time.

15

THE FEELING OF CONTROL

I continued my babysitting jobs throughout high school. There was one family in particular, Charity and Andres, whom I'd worked for continuously for a period of five or so years. They were one of my first jobs, and I grew to adore their kids. I started babysitting for them when I was just nine years old. Andres would drop slightly off-color remarks, which easily passed as a joke. He said, for instance, "You look so cute today I could kiss you." Another time, he teased, "I should leave you for Charity, because you're so good with the kids." Charity, who was often in the room to overhear such remarks would reply with a good-natured, *"Knock it off!"* I never thought anything of it at the time.

Eventually their marriage fell apart and Charity left, taking the kids with her. While Charity relocated closer to town, Andres remained in the house. He always kept his front door open and his house became the place where Wendy Lou, Roger, and I would always hangout. It was almost like a second home to us. Andres would come and go, and said, "Even though Charity's gone, you guys can still hang out here anytime you want." The house remained fully furnished, the lights stayed on, and the house was heated.

Though it wasn't spelled out, in exchange for the use of the house, his liquor cabinet, and all the cigarettes we could smoke, Wendy Lou, who was often my accomplice, and I figured out soon enough what Andres was really after. Andres was hopeful that I would agree to sleep with him. Wendy Lou and I were used to toying with Andres, and holding out on him sexually with the promise of *one day* was an effective tease. Roger never knew what we were up to.

Andres's comments were, by this point, completely unveiled and very bold. Thinking I was a virgin, he would say, "I want to touch you and show you what it is to make love. I can't stop thinking about you, you're so gorgeous." There were many variations on this theme.

Andres also said, "This will feel good; it's something both you and I can enjoy together." Damien never once inquired about my pleasure; it was quite the opposite. He would say, "This will make *me* feel good." Andres's words were surprisingly liberating; I could decide when and if I would be sexual with him, if at all.

Andres knew what my age was, but I passed as an adult, and he treated me as one. Instead of a gangly teenager before him, he saw a woman to be desired and he acted on his adult feelings for me. I implicitly understood that he still saw Wendy Lou as a little girl. There was a difference in how he perceived us.

My interactions with Andres were the first time I realized the potential power I could have over men. I suddenly had sway, and I loved the control I had with Andres. Instead of feeling like the target of unwanted male attention, I now looked for opportunities to turn an attractive man's head. When I got the male attention I sought, it made me feel powerful, beautiful, and unashamed of my body.

16

GOING WEST

When I was fourteen I started spending my summers in Gillette, Wyoming with Patty and Dylan. There was plenty of nightlife there and the bar scene was hopping. Drinking lowered my inhibitions, and I had guys asking me onto the dance floor all the time. I enjoyed my newfound power in getting male attention that I had control over for the first time. When I was drinking, I continued to feel like a better version of myself; someone who was beautiful, flawless, and free of all self-doubt. I often felt no emotional pain and therefore untouchable while drinking; drinking gave me the confidence I didn't have when I was sober. I would continue to use alcohol to medicate all of my feelings in the years to come.

Quint, who was residing in the Black Hills of South Dakota learning the logging business, was just two hours away from Gillette. Quint was a born flirt; he loved women and they loved him. Most girls, when they met him, fell in love with him right away. When he smiled at you, it was as if you were the only woman in the world. He had devastatingly good looks; he was handsome, like my dad.

And he learned every trick in the book from Dad, who always had an easy way with women as well. Like Dad, Quint also had a temper.

As my brothers grew up, Dad's influence over them grew and Dad was always dragging them into the bars. They would play pool, flirt with women, and get into fights. In the bars, if someone stupid was looking for fight, Quint would finish it. He, Dad, and my brothers gained a reputation as the O'Brien gang. Always the big brother, Quint hated when I began drinking, and now that I was fourteen and being treated like an eighteen-year old when I stepped into the bars, *he* stepped in to teach me a lesson. Unlike everyone else, Quint always saw me for my true age. He told me, "If you want to be an adult, then we're going to load up the car with some beer and you're gonna be my bar-hopping partner. Whoever can hold his liquor better gets to party like an adult."

So, with his wife Debbie driving us all over the back roads of South Dakota, we stopped into each and every dive bar. Quint would give me quarters to feed the jukebox, and he wouldn't let any of the guys come too close. We danced to Hank Williams, Johnny Cash, and Waylon Jennings.

We'd stumble out of there and head to the next bar. I conceded when Debbie had to hold my hair back as I puked my guts out in the bathroom of the last bar. I'd lost the bet but it was after that, that Quint started treating me like a friend instead of a baby sister. Debbie later told me, he only won the bet by forty-five minutes.

Spending the rest of that summer with him in the Black Hills of South Dakota remains one of my happiest memories. Quint and I would idle away the lazy summer days. We worked on his cars and trucks while listening to Cat Stevens. There were a lot of car rides exploring the exceptional natural beauty of the hills. Taking in deep inhalations, which were infused with the smell of the surrounding pine trees, it was the freshest air I would ever breathe.

17

GONE TOO SOON

By the time I was fourteen, I started confiding in my mom as if we were friends. Being a naturally quiet person, she was the perfect confidant and was always available to lend an ear. I told her everything: the hate I had for Dad, and the love I had for Roger.

Unlike my sexually explicit experiences with Damien, in which I dissociated often, I was so in love with Roger that I had to be present for all of it. I didn't want to miss a moment of shared intimacy with him. I found Roger beautiful, every part of him. I could look at his hands and admire them for hours. I had Roger to pour all my love into and it was my saving grace.

Being with Roger, there was never any pressure on me to have sex at all. On the occasions when our physical closeness would lead to making love, it was a shared experience. Having sex with Damien was all about feeding the monster. While Damien was reaching his sexual peak at eighteen, I was being violated almost daily. In contrast, when Roger made love to me I would feel his soul. While Roger could sense turmoil in me, he thought it had to do with my turbulent relationship with my dad and my mom's prolonged illness. Sensing when I was upset, he was always there for me whenever I needed him. He never knew that Damien was violating me, and I clung to Roger as my lifeline.

By a cruel twist of fate, the very next day after we'd both agreed to date each other exclusively, and to break off ties with the other people we were dating, he was taken from me. When I got to school the following day after we'd made our promises, he wasn't there though we'd agreed to meet. I had a secret of my own to tell him; I believed that I was pregnant. I was only going to tell him once I knew we were going to be together for the long-term. I spent the whole school day feeling unsettled. I couldn't wait to hear his explanation.

Getting off the school bus that day, Damien's girlfriend ran up to me completely hysterical, shouting, "Roger's dead." I remember looking at her, seeing her face, caked with makeup, just hating her for saying such a despicable thing. Choosing not to believe a word, I pushed my way past her and ran into the house looking for my mom, and searching for answers.

I found my mom sitting in her recliner crying. Looking at her tear-stained cheeks, I knew it was true. Roger was gone; my true love was gone. My knees gave out, and I collapsed alongside her, a pile of tears.

I begged her to tell me it wasn't true, sobbing uncontrollably. My mom kept saying she was so sorry, stroking my hair. I could tell by my mom's eyes she understood my pain, and felt it as her own.

Because so much of my whole life was lived with Roger, and for Roger, my whole life as I knew it was over. To this day, I can't put words to the pain I felt coursing through me. It was my first time losing someone who was so dear to me to death. I couldn't breathe, knowing the future I'd dreamed about for years was shattered.

When Wendy Lou called, I ran to my friend, knowing she needed me. When we saw each other we held each other and cried our eyes out. Roger was not only her brother, but truly a good friend too. We were three, and now we were two. His absence would always be felt.

Wendy Lou explained to me what had taken place that morning at their house. Roger had decided to go to work with his Dad instead of going to school. He was cutting branches down near power lines and his chainsaw came down on one of the lines, electrocuting him. His heart stopped, and he died instantly of cardiac arrest.

I was racked with guilt and kept Roger's promise to share a future with me a secret from her for years. I believed at that time that Roger chose to skip school that day to avoid any messy emotional confrontations. I couldn't tell her until years later, that I felt responsible for killing him. It was one more secret I felt I had to keep, and buried it deep inside of me.

Roger's viewing was a few days later, I had to borrow a dress from Wendy's Mom because I didn't have anything to wear. The whole school showed up to pay their respects; he was that popular. Walking in, Roger's mom was the first person I made eye contact with. She held my gaze, and without saying a word, she acknowledged my deep love for her son. It was the first time she'd included me in such a way.

The walk up to his casket was the hardest thing I ever did up to that point in my life. On trembling legs, I prepared to say my last goodbye. The body looked nothing like my Roger. I convinced myself it wasn't him, as it didn't look like him at all. I saw nothing of the youthful face of the boy I loved.

I tried to go to the funeral but, in unbearable emotional pain, I wasn't yet prepared to face the reality of his death. I was still in shock. Going to his funeral would have been an acknowledgement that he was really gone and I wasn't ready to lose him, so I didn't. It took Wendy Lou a long time before she could forgive me for not going to Roger's funeral.

Not long after Roger's death, I started cramping and buckled over, racked in pain. I estimated I was four months into my pregnancy. Getting myself to a bathroom, blood started pouring out of me and I felt a huge blood clot fall out. My worst fear was that I was miscarrying Roger's and my baby. I looked in the toilet and saw an unformed fetus. I couldn't believe I had lost the only thing I had left of Roger. I was completely destroyed inside. I was intent on raising his child, and losing our baby was like losing him all over again. I never told anyone, not even Wendy Lou.

I started using alcohol to self-medicate. I was in so much emotional pain after losing Roger and our unborn baby. I always had plenty of access to my dad's beer, but I started to need something stronger. Damien was more than willing to get me the strong stuff as long as I paid for it with my babysitting money. I drank E&J brandy as it was the cheapest. In the months after Roger died, I drank every day. After coming home from school each day, I'd have my first drink. By nightfall, I was pretty drunk and my goal was to drink enough to pass out each night.

Wendy Lou was worried about me, and told me I was drinking way too much. But I just couldn't seem to let her in, I was hurting too much and wallowing in my own private pain. I knew she was hurting too in the aftermath of her brother's death. I was glad she had the support of new friends she'd made at school. In contrast, the few friends I'd made at school, I pushed away. Though Wendy Lou and I remained friends, I continued to isolate myself.

I used to throw all my booze bottles in the field in the long grass by the house to hide them. Standing from my front porch, I would chuck my empty bottles as far as I could into the long grass. When spring came the following year, the field was littered with all my booze bottles. I think even my dad was shocked to see how much I had drank.

18

RAGE

I was the last kid living at home; after Roger's death, I felt like I had been cheated. I had so much anger inside of me, it started to corrode within me. I had no sense of control over my life and I also had no freedom to live my life as I would have liked. I was in an emotional tailspin, and I was at my breaking point. My dad had become completely intolerable. His drinking was making him permanently mean.

When my older siblings came into town to visit Mom, as she got progressively sicker, The Old Man would instigate fights to the point of frustrating his kids that they would have to leave prematurely. My mom, who was quite frail, would be crying silent tears as they departed. She loved her kids and wanted the comfort of her children around her during these final years of her life. I would remain behind and observe how much she suffered because of my father's reckless and foolish behavior. My anger boiled down into a deep-seated rage. I hated that she just let Dad walk all over her. In stark contrast, she was always defending him.

Among her excuses for him were:

"He's had such a rough life."

My thoughts that went unsaid were:
*Why is he torturing me in the same way? Wouldn't a father
want **better** for his own kids?*

"That's just the way he is."
*He's that way because of his drinking. He drinks to escape his
past.*

"You always stand by your man."
You deserve better. I will never let a man control me like this.

"It could be worse."
What could be worse than this?

With my dad drinking beer and brandy everyday, it was
only a matter of time before I ended up doing the same.
One day, when we were both drunk, we had a heated
exchange of words. Both my dad and I had all this rage
inside of us and we were like two magnets. By this point,
Roger had died and all my unexpressed rage I felt in losing
him was ready to explode.

"You're still a drunk and still treat Mom horribly, even
though she is sick," I threw the words in his face.

Now I'd gotten him pissed I was really able to get under
his skin. He countered with, "I know you and that Roger
were fooling around and you got knocked up. I made sure
you didn't have that baby, didn't I?"

I froze. I always suspected he knew I was pregnant.
During that time, he had me lifting all of the big logs that he
usually did himself. I tried making excuses not to lift them,
but he had me lift them anyway.

Hearing his admission, I flew into a rage. He'd just
admitted to killing my baby. So I went after him. I threw

punches that never landed and he aggressively pushed me back. I nearly fell down the basement stairs.

My mom was upstairs in her chair listening to everything as it unfolded. I screamed at him, "I'll never forgive you for that! I hate you! I know you cheat on Mom and you're a fucking asshole!" I ran up the stairs and stopped to comfort my mother, who was crying. I apologized for what she'd just overheard. Even if she knew about Dad's infidelities, it's never something that we'd have said aloud. She responded, "Don't worry. I'm okay."

I was consumed with rage that he'd played a role in my miscarriage. I'd had some of my mom's pain pills stockpiled, as she always had extra. In my room that night, I smoked some pot to calm down, and then washed down a whole bunch of her pills with brandy. I was ready to die. I wanted to be with Roger again so badly and I couldn't handle the separation I was enduring. I didn't want to hurt my mom but I was drowning in my own pain. As I laid down on my bed, I looked at the unicorn bed sheets Quint had bought me for my sixteenth birthday. Of all my siblings, I was always the closest to my protective older brother Quint.

As my head started feeling woozy, I apologized to Quint, and then my eyelids got heavier and heavier. I couldn't keep my eyes open. A whooshing sound reverberated through my ears and brought with it a heavy darkness. Paralysis akin to a heavy weighted blanket set in and I started to get scared discovering that I couldn't move a muscle. I tried to get up but couldn't, then I tried calling for my mom but couldn't talk. I was in the hazy dream state between being just barely awake before dropping off into an abyss of sleep. I started to struggle and fought the feeling.

I became terrified because I suddenly knew if I gave in to the heaviness I wouldn't be waking up. I thought I had sealed my fate, and my life's story was ending here. This was the last act. Incredibly, I did wake up the next day and I vowed I'd never make an attempt on my life ever again no matter how bad things got. I was going to fight for my life.

My suicide attempt was my emotional rock bottom. Waking up surprised that God spared my life after I'd taken what was a lethal amount of pills and booze, I wasted no time in leaving behind the hell I'd been enduring. I got up and packed a bag, ignored my Dad, kissed my Mom goodbye and went to school. I told my school counselor I wouldn't be in school anymore. I got a seat on the next flight to Jackson.

When I got to my sister Caitlyn's house, I called my mom and told her I was sorry for worrying her but that I wasn't coming home. She said she understood. Caitlyn took me in, no questions asked, and I lived with her for a full year. I was scared, nervous, and excited; I had my second chance. During that time, with Caitlyn's loving support, I didn't drink at all. The compulsion was gone; I didn't need to.

I had just left a world where I was drowning my grief in alcohol. I was starting a new life here, where no one knew me. I reinvented myself. As much as I loved Roger, I knew I had to accept he was gone and move on with my life. I stopped daydreaming and fantasizing that he was alive.

Jackson, Michigan was such a big city with so many people and roads. Detroit and Ann Arbor were neighboring cities. Caitlyn made sure I had everything I needed so that I would fit in. The best thing she ever bought me was contacts. Glasses made me feel ugly.

I started my junior year of high school nervous but hopeful. Caitlyn introduced me to her friend's daughter, Candy, who was very popular. I had a free pass to all the normal teenaged activities and I participated in them all. I had newfound freedoms, and I never knew school could be so fun. I was a straight A student, living the best year of my life.

I was a carefree kid, going to movies, enjoying school dances, and joining team sports for the first time in my life. While neither basketball nor volleyball were my strongest suit, being part of a team improved my morale. My favorite activity was roller skating on the weekends at a rink that was decked out with music and disco lights.

My friends and I would drive around the main drag of Jackson like all the other kids our age. In an effort to impress all the cute boys, we spent time carefully doing our clothes, makeup, and hair.

I planned on going to college. I wanted to see more of the world, and thought maybe I'd pursue a career as a flight attendant. It was hectic living with Caitlyn and her husband Wayne and their four boys in such a small house, but we made it work. I helped Caitlyn with raising the boys, and she gave me the love and support that enabled me to be a happy teenager. Her husband Wayne was also a stabilizing force in my life.

19

STAND BY YOUR MAN

I met Logan on my seventeenth birthday. He was drop dead gorgeous with a charming smile that never left his face. He reminded me of Roger and I soon fell head over heels in love for the second time in my life. He had me so enthralled with him.

Logan said he was twenty-one and residing in his own apartment, and that he had a car and a job. He also said he played in a band. I thought that was badass, but it turns out that none of it was true; he was a pathological liar.

At first, I thought no big deal. When I found out he didn't have an apartment as he'd claimed, again, it was no big deal. We found other places with friends to hang out. When I found out he had no car and no job, I let both of those slide too.

After Roger died, I didn't fall in love again until Logan. In some ways, I was trying to find my way back to Roger and when I met Logan, who shared some superficial similarities with a boy I'd loved so entirely, I became quickly attached. In actuality, the two were fundamentally nothing alike. Roger, who I grew up alongside and who I knew since the age of seven had ambition and the promise of a bright future, whereas Logan lived day to day and had no aspirations to call his own.

I told Caitlyn I'd met someone new and she was so happy for me and couldn't wait to meet my new stud. She cautioned me to go slow. But Me... go slow?! NOT! I had to be with him every day, as I skipped past every red flag imaginable. Caitlyn hated the fact that he was unemployed. Eventually meeting him, she was unimpressed and thought of him as lazy.

Caitlyn's low opinion of Logan never changed and she said she didn't think I should see Logan anymore. Caitlyn wanted me to see the world and all it had to offer; she believed I could accomplish anything I set my mind to. She feared that Logan would hold me back from achieving my true potential. Caitlyn, who is ten years my senior, was more like a second mother to me. Her forbidding me to see Logan wasn't going to work for me. I'd convinced myself I was in L-O-V-E and nobody was going to stop me. I'd just finished my junior year in high school and had a full-time job as a nanny. I had some money saved up, so, Logan and I decided we'd elope in Nashville to get married.

The night we left for Nashville, I wrote a note to Caitlyn telling her that I loved her but had to follow my heart. Logan and I hitchhiked with truck drivers and arrived in Nashville broke but happy. We went to the courthouse and were turned away when we found out that I wasn't able to be legally married until I was eighteen, and I was a year shy of the mark. When Logan and I returned to Jackson, my sense of pride kept me from revealing the truth to Caitlyn. I told her I was a married woman, though I wasn't, because I wanted her to accept Logan.

With just the clothes on our backs and twenty dollars to our name, we hitchhiked back up to Michigan. I had a bottomless well of patience for Logan and told myself that catching him in petty lies wasn't as important as the love he professed for me regularly. Without a place to stay, we stayed on a friend's couch for a few days, and after that, we slept on the streets and shoplifted for our food. We would walk around all day looking for returnable cans to recycle.

Sometimes being out in the open made me feel vulnerable and scared but we had each other. I also felt a sense of freedom I hadn't felt in a long time. Our only worry was finding food and a place to sleep. I was still so wrapped up in my love for Logan, that nothing else mattered than being with him. I felt fortunate that the feelings were mutual.

While living on the streets, Caitlyn would pick me up and feed me, but not Logan. She would watch me eat every bite so I wouldn't save anything for Logan. By this point, she really hated Logan and had a lot of contempt for him, still believing that he was ruining my life. I could have gone back to Caitlyn's house at any time, but I couldn't desert Logan.

By the end of summer, Mom and Dad came down to Jackson after Caitlyn reached out to them. They were concerned and stepped in. I had a sense of dread seeing my dad again. It was the first encounter I'd have with him, since our big blowout months before. I was shocked to see how frail my mom looked. She was in horrible shape, seeing that her condition had worsened. My mom begged me to come home and finish high school, and I told her I wouldn't go without Logan. My dad said, "Logan can work on wood with me, for your room and board, while you finish school." I think my dad felt guilty about what had happened between us and this was his way of apologizing. I tried warning Logan how controlling my dad could be.

When I left home the year before and had decided to move in with Caitlyn, I didn't know at the time when I'd be back at the farm, if ever. When I did return to the farm, it was with Logan in tow, and in September I returned to school for twelfth grade. I completed my final year of high school on time and graduated.

Upon my return I stayed by Mom's side everyday. I would make her favorite meal of scrambled eggs, but she could barely eat them. Still, I could tell she loved having me back home. I felt a terrible guilt for having left her with only my dad when I so desperately needed the change, which living with Caitlyn made possible. My mom's leukemia treatments were taking a visible toll on her, and she was losing weight quickly.

After a short stay on the farm, when Dad started fighting again with me, and now Logan, I knew it was time to move into our own place. In some ways Dad and I were so alike; both of us had unresolved anger in us and explosive tempers which were always on display becoming a great burden to my mom's peace of mind. Mom never made me feel guilty for moving off the farm with Logan.

I made sure to call her everyday. We'd talk about how she was feeling, and she was always curious to know how Logan and I were doing. I noticed she always waited to hear from me, rather than picking the phone herself to call and say hello. When I asked her why she did this she told me, "Parents shouldn't have to call their kids. My kids have their own lives and if any of them are thinking about me, they'll call me."

As my mother became progressively more sick, Dad was often in the bars chasing women. He was running away from the prospect that he was going to be losing the love of his wife to death. The companion who had faithfully been by his side for over forty years was dying. It was almost as if Dad was wasting no time trying to replace Mom's role in his life. He could never handle being alone and always needed a woman by his side. His actions in the last year of my mom's life seemed utterly despicable but he was reacting out of sheer panic and a sense of helplessness. When the doctors told him that every experimental leukemia treatment had been exhausted in the attempts to extend my mother's life, his carousing and heavy drinking became an outward sign of his deep grief.

Dad and I started butting heads a lot as we saw my mom waste away during the final rounds of her chemotherapy treatments. The resentment I had for him only grew when I saw his total neglect in caring for Mom. I could find no excuses for him, when I saw how he was consistently putting his drinking life before family. I often had to scour all the bars in South Range, and when I found him, I'd raise enough hell, sufficiently pissing him off and getting him out of the bar at the same time. On those days, I felt like I'd won that hand. It was a mental game of poker.

If my mom wasn't going to demand his attention during her sickest and weakest moments, I was going to demand it for her. It was so ironic because growing up he'd always told us, "We always help each other in this family." Here he was seeming to do the exact opposite. To me, it looked like he was abandoning Mom, who had lived every day of her life as a pacifier who'd kept us all together.

20

MY MIRACLE BABY

I woke up one morning sick to my stomach and it dawned on me that I hadn't started my period. I was on the pill, so I wasn't too worried. Then I was sick again the next couple of mornings. I called my Mom, and she said since I was a pill baby, I should get a pregnancy test.

Oh, shit, was my first thought. I didn't want a kid. Me, a mother? I couldn't even take care of myself. How would Logan and I be able to raise a kid? Logan said it would be okay and that if I was pregnant, he would step up and be a father. After the test confirmed I was pregnant, Logan and I looked at each other and we both broke out with big smiles. It was a happy moment for us, as we wrapped our heads around the idea of being young parents. I called my mom right away and she started crying she was so happy for me and she said, "I always wanted to see you become a mother."

As soon as I knew Joey was on the way, my motherly instincts kicked in right away. Logan showed no initiative or any signs that he would be capable of holding down a job. Him knowing that he would be a father one day in the near future did nothing to light a fire under his feet. A witness to his apathy, I reasoned that I was going to go it alone. Being closer to home I was fortunate I had the support of my mom, Caitlin, Patty, and Wendy Lou. They gave me resolve and I did everything in my power to prepare for my child's birth.

Patty helped me get my own apartment and I began to nest. As busy as she was with her own kids, Patty always found time for me. I worked four part-time jobs continuously through my eighth month of pregnancy. I was determined to have a financial nest egg for after my child was born.

I loved every moment of being pregnant. As soon as I could feel Joey moving within me, I started engaging him. I'd talk to him, read books aloud, and played music against my belly. I wanted to give my child the whole world. He would grow up to be mine, and would help redefine me in new ways that gave me a deep understanding of unconditional love. The bond I have with my first child is a connection that remains an unbroken cord to this day.

During a routine ultrasound in my eighth month, my doctors found a serious anomaly which terrified me. My baby had water in both his brain and lungs and a heart valve which looked smaller and underdeveloped. They immediately headed down state to Ann Arbor, MI, where I could get a reputable second opinion.

I stayed with Caitlyn and her family again, as they lived near Ann Arbor, and vigilantly kept up with my ultrasounds twice a week. Though I was surrounded by the love of family leading up to the last month, I felt alone and scared at the prospect of giving birth to a child who would need so much extra care. I had every intention to care for my child whatever his needs would be; this was my pledge.

The doctors in Ann Arbor confirmed what my hometown doctor first detected. My child might be born with brain damage and he would have congenital heart problems. They elected not to do any invasive procedures while Joey was still in utero, and the doctors wanted to wait until our official due date to induce me.

While I was away from the Upper Peninsula, Patty took on the role of being my eyes and ears. She heard rumors that Logan was less than faithful. Going to confront Logan, whom I'd allowed to move back in with me when he again found himself with no place to stay, Patty found Logan and the other woman in my apartment. Patty is not someone to hold anything back, and things came to blows. She physically threw both of them out that very afternoon. When Patty broke the news to me, I was truly heartbroken. I was back to square one and felt totally alone in the world.

I prayed to God, "If I could have my baby, I could be strong enough to make it through this heartbreak." The next day I went to my ultrasound and the water was gone! My baby's underdeveloped heart valve was suddenly normal. The doctors were mystified. The reputable team of healthcare professionals had no answers for me; they couldn't explain the miracle. I know what happened; God had fixed my baby.

Two days later, prior to my due date, I was crying again, telling God, "I need my baby." As I was talking to God, my water broke, and I was elated. I was going to meet my son! I was induced after my water broke following visible signs of a bloody show and I was in labor for twelve hours. The contractions were horrible. After five minutes of pushing, my son's heart rate started plummeting fast.

My baby was in distress and I was rushed to the operating room for an emergency c-section. I felt unheard as I tried to grapple with what was happening. It was pandemonium. They were losing the fetal heartbeat and just moments before I was given anesthesia, I heard the doctor say, "The baby has no heartbeat." I went to sleep thinking my son was dead.

While I was under, I had lucid dreams of walking through a vast flat space, surrounded by a foggy white mist, in a field that stretched out infinitely. I would hear my son's cries, and as I'd run in his direction, getting close to where I thought he was, he would disappear before I could reach him. I'd then hear his cries elsewhere and the same frantic search would begin again.

Caitlyn was by my side throughout my labor and delivery, encouraging me and holding my hand the whole time. After Joey was delivered, I was unresponsive to their attempts to wake me. Somehow Caitlyn, who was a mother herself, knew instinctively that the doctors needed to get my son into my arms. She was ignored until my heartrate could be stabilized. They told Caitlyn my life was on the line, and she shouted again, "You'd better get her son into her arms, quick, so that she knows Joey is alive."

Do you believe in miracles?

When I opened my eyes and saw Joey in my arms for the first time, everything in my life made sense. God had kept his promise to me. Joey was born healthy and was the most beautiful baby I'd ever set my eyes on. He was mine. I thought I'd lost him and that he had died, and now here I was holding him. Having him in my arms was pure bliss.

The doctors did every kind of test there was. Scratching their heads, the doctors had no way to explain how Joey was born healthy; he was a medical mystery. He was truly my miracle baby. He took to breastfeeding right away and slept on my chest every night. We were safely discharged from the hospital, and we stayed at Caitlyn's house while the stitches from my cesarean were healing.

21

WILL YOU MARRY ME?

Everyone was eager to see Joey, especially my mother who was so elated at the initial news of my pregnancy. My mom believed that being a mother was the most cherished role in a woman's life. She was visibly weak but was so excited to meet her grandson. As she rocked Joey in her arms it was an incredibly emotional moment for me. She said, "He's so beautiful." I felt like I'd given her an incredible gift.

My Mom loved being a grandmother. Perhaps because she didn't have the pressure that comes with motherhood. She was always holding our babies; and showered them with the devotion that was lost on us when we were younger. It always surprised Patty, Caitlyn, and me to see her playing with her grandkids so affectionately and taking the time to read with them.

After Joey's birth, Quint came from South Dakota to see his nephew and fell in love with Joey right away, as we all did. I was so happy to see Quint again; my older brother was always able to make me feel like I mattered. Upon hearing that my relationship with Logan was on the rocks, Quint tried convincing me to move to South Dakota where he could keep a brotherly eye on me. Part of me wanted to start a new life but I couldn't imagine leaving Mom again.

After I'd healed from the sutures from my cesarean, Joey and I prepared to return to the Upper Peninsula. Without Logan, it would be me and Joey against the world. I was determined to provide for my son, and I accepted every cash job I could get my hands on. Joey was well cared for and my basic needs were met. There was a roof over our head, and I was making it work.

Logan wanted to see his son. As his father, I felt he had a right to see Joey. Though news of his infidelity proved to me he was no longer trustworthy or deserving of my love, I reluctantly let Logan come and see his son. Seeing Logan with Joey made me realize how much Joey would benefit with a father in his life. Logan was wise to this and soon after began asking me to marry him. He instinctively knew that my highest goal was having my own family.

My mom kept after me to forgive Logan for his infidelity and to get married. After I learned about my father's many infidelities while married to Mom, I wanted my married life to be different. I didn't want the same fate. I found it hard to forgive Logan, in the same way I never forgave my father. I was stubborn and thought I didn't need a man in my life. I told her as much, believing Joey was the only one I needed. But Mom was very insistent. She said she wanted to see me settled and for Joey to grow up with a father in his life.

A couple months later, I received a call from the Army recruiter's office; the officer on the phone told me, "I'm sitting here with Logan Redding, and he's just signed up for the army ma'am." He was blunt and to the point when he next asked, "*Will you marry this man, now?*" I could hear a crowd of male voices hooting and hollering in the background.

I had my reservations and asked, "Well, did he actually sign the papers?" The officer, with his strong Southern drawl confirmed, "Yes, Ma'am." Logan had been asking me the same question for months, and I'd always turned him down. But that day, when Logan got on the phone, he charmed me with promises of a new and improved life together. I finally said yes.

Logan and I got married in November at Dylan and Patty's house when Joey was about three months old. All of my family was there and everybody seemed happy for us except Caitlyn. On my wedding day, I had mixed feelings about getting married and I was actually in tears. I couldn't deny that I had cold feet. My mom, who barely had enough strength to get up Patty's stairs, came and sat by me to console me.

She took my hands and looked at me with this pleading look in her eyes. She said, "Please do this for your son. He needs a father and Logan is a good man. He just needs a little coaxing. I need to know you and Joey will be okay." Even Logan's parents attended the wedding. I looked up and saw Logan's mom holding Joey standing just outside our door overhearing my mom's plea. I dried my eyes, and said aloud, "How bad can it be?"

22

COUNTRY BUMPKIN

BY CAL SMITH

One afternoon following a particularly harsh chemotherapy treatment which left my mom feeling so nauseated, she needed to get home and into a bed right away. The Old Man, however, refused to interrupt his afternoon of drinking and carousing in order to attend to her.

I stormed into the bar intent on getting my Dad off his barstool when I found him flirting with a younger woman named Leah, who he would eventually date. Leah knew my Dad was married and my Mom had cancer, but she didn't care. I wanted to punch her lights out.

Furiously, I wedged my way in between the two of them, and said, "Your wife is done with her cancer treatment and she's terribly sick. She needs to get home *right now*."

He responded, "I'll leave when I'm ready, Daughter. Mind your own business." He was a full-fledged alcoholic by this point, finding any reason to go to the bars. In denial about so many things, he defended his poor choices by saying, "I control my drinking." He was a control freak in many aspects of his life, but he obviously couldn't control his drinking. Hours later, on his own timetable, he finally got into the truck, where Mom was still waiting, and drove them both home. My mom was in the last months of her life.

Mom's chemotherapy treatments would soon stop when the doctors felt additional chemo was no longer necessary. There were no more treatment options; she'd tried them all. She continued to fight the leukemia so hard; she was living for her family now. We didn't know if it was a matter of weeks or a matter of just days. Throughout her trials, mom stubbornly stood by her man and found no fault with The Old Man. She continued to make excuses for him until the very end.

In her final months, all of my brothers and Caitlyn came home for the holidays. We gathered at the farm to be with her. As always she was seated in her favorite chair, the brown recliner that was so lived in. Just outside her window was the bird feeder that my dad made sure to always keep filled. Chickadees, blue jays, and woodpeckers were her constant companions; these birds would not migrate south and were there all year. The spacious living room, where we set up our Christmas tree, was where she spent the majority of her days watching her favorite television programs.

Her eyes are tired and hollowed out from her many years of battling leukemia, but she wore a weak smile for her kids and grandkids, whom she loved having around. Her family was her pride and joy. While all of my other siblings had come to grips with accepting that she wouldn't be around for much longer, I, on the other hand, refused to accept the stark reality of the truth.

As her illness progressed, she was admitted to Marquette Memorial in the final month of her life. Quint, who always had a very strong bond with our mother, came up from South Dakota and he and I made the two hour drive from Donken to be by her side. After seeing her, Quint and I were both in tears as we helped each other accept that our Mom was going to die. We held onto each other the whole way back. This would be the last time Quint saw her. As fate would have it, it was also the last time that I saw Quint.

Just a few weeks later, Quint got caught up in a snowstorm when his truck went missing. Mom was beside herself crying; she was so distraught that no one could find her son. Much to everyone's relief, his truck was recovered, and Quint called his mom after being treated at the hospital for frostbite and other minor injuries.

A week before my mom died, I was in her room at the hospital and we had a candid talk about death and dying. I asked if she was scared, and she said, "A little." Because of my parents' belief in the spiritual realm, both Mom and Dad believed death was a transition and not an end. She said, "I'm going to be by his side. I'm always going to be with your dad." I asked her if she would give me a sign after she died to let me know she was okay. She said she didn't want to scare me and I told her she wouldn't. I needed to know that she was still there in spirit.

I took ahold of her hand and asked her if she had anything she wanted to tell me. She looked at me, her once bright blue eyes which now took on a cloudy hue, and said, "Family always comes first. Always be there for each other and help your dad."

She loved my dad more than she loved us. While she would never admit to this, her actions always spoke louder than her words. After my mom died, all I could think about were her words to me before she died, "Take care of your dad."

She told me how happy she was that I married Logan and said, "Seeing you with Joey, you're so great with him. I know how much you adore him. You'll be a better mom than me."

"You're a wonderful mom!" I responded.

"I've always loved you kids so much, but I never knew how to show it properly." It seemed like my mom was expressing her last regrets. She wished she could have expressed more physical affection for us.

I offered the quiet support that she often lent me. But as a new mother, I had fears and I confided in my mother before she passed away, "I don't know how to be a good mom without your help." She offered some reassuring words by saying, "You have your sister and Patty; they are good moms and you will be too." It was the kindest thing my mom ever told me, and it gave me the strength to move forward.

I got to see her one last time after that. She was eating and drinking again, and looked so good. Seeing her revived, I got my hopes up thinking she was really going to beat the odds once again. She told me that she wasn't done fighting yet. She even told Caitlyn to go on a planned family vacation to Florida and that she was fine.

Two days later, on February 14th, I received a call at 2:03 in the morning; it was from my mom's nurse, who said, "I'm sorry, but your mother has just passed away."

"She was fine, I just saw her two days ago."

"Sometimes it happens this way. Patients show signs of getting better and are able to say goodbye to their loved ones before they go."

"Is my father there? Was he with her when she died?"

"No, he wasn't."

Upon hearing this, it broke my heart because every fiber of my body knew he was at the bar. My mom was alone when she took her last breath.

Joey was just seven months at the time and Logan was in South Carolina in basic training. I was living two hours away in South Range. I remember calling Dylan first and telling him that Mom died. That's all I said to him before hanging up. The pain was so great that I could barely breathe. I wanted to scream knowing that my family would never be the same again. She quietly connected all the branches of our family tree. I went out of my body. I dissociated and went to a place far away where the pain couldn't reach me. It was an automatic response to the enormity of my grief. I had recently lost Roger, and the pain of now also losing my mother was too much to bear.

Two and a half hours later, hearing Joey cry for his bottle roused me. It was two and a half hours that I couldn't account for. I know I was not asleep, but I have no memories of where inside of myself I had retreated to during my dissociation. As soon as I came to, I found a coping mechanism that I used to help me deal with all the loss I was feeling. I concocted a fantasy, just as I did with Roger, fantasizing that he was still alive and well out there somewhere. I told myself Mom was okay, still in her hospital bed, and just two hours away in Marquette. This shunted the pain.

I wouldn't answer my phone for days, because I knew what everyone would say, and I didn't want to believe the reality of the news just yet. *I needed time to pretend.* And that's just what I did. It was easy for me to pretend she was still alive. It was a couple of years before I could even talk about the loss of my mother. Our family would endure more unbearable losses to come.

My dad insisted that there be no funeral or wake for my mother. We didn't put anything in the paper. Nothing. It was as if her passing away didn't even happen. While my dad said those were her wishes and that they'd made the decision together, we wondered if this was truly her last wish. Or was he controlling her up until the very end?

The peacemaker who'd kept our family together for so many years died relatively young, at fifty-one. She endured so much strife throughout her life, but everything she did or didn't do was in service of her family. She met and fell in love with a man who she was fiercely committed to throughout her life, giving him five children. She did the best she knew how with everything life had dealt her. I was never certain if she ever knew what her son Damien was capable of. Whatever she knew, if she knew, passed away with her.

After my Mom died in February, Quint was devastated by the loss because there was a particularly strong bond between Mom and him, perhaps because Dad always singled out Quint for the harshest punishments. I believe his grief was getting the best of him; he probably wasn't getting enough sleep and was most likely drinking too much.

Just after Mom's death, I got a phone call from Quint, who loved being an uncle to Joey. He asked me and Joey to come stay with him in South Dakota for a while saying to me, "I'll help you with Joey. We'll help each other. I'm having a really hard time and need you." I wanted to go, however, being newly married, Logan, who was struggling getting through Basic Training, relied heavily on me for emotional support. Logan whined that he didn't want me and Joey to go, and my mom's words to 'stand by your man' rang in my ears. I've realized in hindsight that I made the wrong choice by staying put. When I called Quint and told him Joey and I weren't coming, I'll never forget the defeat I heard in his voice. It was the last time I heard his voice.

23

ARMY LIFE / LOST IN THE TIMBER

The spring after my mom died, Logan had completed basic training and my Dad helped Logan, Joey, and I move to Watertown, NY where Logan was newly stationed. We put all we owned into a small wood trailer and hitched it to Dad's old truck. We pulled up at the military base after two days.

Almost as soon as we arrived, in true Old Man style, my dad jumped back into his truck and wished me farewell, saying, "Good luck Daughter, love you." That's when it hit me that this was the first time I'd be living so far removed from family. Even while I was living on the streets in Jackson, I was only a few miles from Caitlyn who stayed very involved. Not knowing what was ahead of me, I wanted to cry, watching my dad leave. Feeling truly alone, I clung to my son like a life preserver.

My dad did what he always did when dealing with his own private pain, he took off. He got a woman, stayed drunk, and traveled. Dad was nothing without the adoration of a female companion. My mother suffered in silence through his many infidelities while she was alive, and after her death, he resumed his womanizing ways. We didn't see him for another three months.

Army life was a rude awakening. We had to stay in the barracks in adjoining rooms with other families. I was frightened with all these other strangers around. There was zero privacy. The housing situation was organized chaos and was very disorienting. Joey wasn't breastfeeding, so I had to figure out how to get water for his formula and how to warm up his food. I found myself asking, *What had we signed up for?*

This went on for about a month. Joey and I ate in the mess hall with a bunch of strangers. I was socially awkward, and didn't make friends very easily, which only added to my feelings of loneliness. It seemed as if I didn't see Logan very much at all. Some of his training exercises would last for weeks at a time. With no transportation and no money, Joey and I were incredibly isolated. Money was tight, as we only got paid once a month.

After a month, we finally moved into a different barracks with our own room. It was basically a motel room with a bed and a bathroom and a little stove and fridge. It was a huge relief to finally have some privacy and we settled in for the next six months.

When we finally got paid, I had to be very careful on how we spent our money. I bought our food at the commissary and always bought too much formula and baby food because I was scared of running out.

And then, grief found me again. Logan and I had just gotten back from celebrating my birthday dinner. Residing in a motel residence the army had arranged for our accommodations, there was a long hallway with pay phones. A neighboring stranger knocked on my door and told me I'd received a phone call. Picking up the dangling receiver from the pay phone, I discovered it was Dylan. He was trying too hard to be funny. Having been separated from my family for months, I remember getting excited at the prospect that he and Patty were in town on a surprise visit. My first time away from home, as a new mom, and as a relatively new wife, I was terribly homesick. I missed everyone so badly. Having moved to New York right after my mom passed away made the separation even harder.

"Are you and Patty here!?"

There was a long pause. I sensed something was wrong. And then Dylan said softly, "We lost Quint."

"Where is he?" I replied.

"We. Lost. Quint." Dylan said again.

"Well, where is he?" I was confused.

In my mind, Quint was just missing, perhaps lost in another snowstorm. It was just a couple months earlier, before Mom died, when Quint's truck slid down a ravine. He wasn't found for days. In fact, he almost died *then*, if a fellow logger hadn't spotted his flickering headlights Quint would have frozen to death for sure. Quint had so many near fatal accidents, we'd teased him often and said he had nine lives.

I repeated myself, "*Well, where is he*? In the mountains again?" I was awaiting my brother's reply; there was a long pause on the other end of the phone call.

"No. Not this time. This time we lost him. He died."

The rest of what Dylan told me was a blur. He said something about calling Caitlyn to hurry home. Hearing none of what he said, I said 'okay' and hung up the phone. I wanted to call Quint and tell him this wasn't funny. In complete shock, I went back to my room and held Joey close in my arms all night. I didn't even tell Logan until the next day. Two days later we flew to Jackson, MI where I met up with Caitlyn. Once there, we drove up to the Upper Peninsula.

Quint had returned home, where his final resting place would be. Dylan refused to let any of us see Quint because his body was so disfigured. Wanting to see my brother one last time, Dylan's refusal made me confront the circumstances of his death, as I was roused from my shock.

Quint was driving his skidder on the mountain, a work vehicle that removed the debris of the tree stumps before the timber could be accessed. On a steep slope, for whatever reason, he lost control of the skidder, though he was a seasoned logger. He wasn't paying attention and the skidder rolled all the way down the mountain; he was crushed.

When Dad got news of Quint's death, he returned to the farm and stayed on for a while afterwards. Everyone could see losing both his wife and son took a toll on him; my dad was at a complete loss. Without Quint and Mom, who died within three months of each other, our family drifted in a sea of heartbreak.

The fresh loss left me in a trance-like shock. I was completely numb and there were no tears. One way to retain my sanity during a time of such great grief was to redirect any thoughts of loss almost as soon as I conceived of them. Mom and Quint were alive and well. They were fine. During the funeral, I continued to feel like a zombie, there but not there. I was peering in from the outside.

Suddenly, I came to my senses when I was at his grave site, and then all I wanted to do was scream and scream. The grief struck me like a tsunami. All of us O'Briens were there, in disbelief that we were burying another one of our own just a mere three months after losing our mom. Quint and Mom were the two people who were always the guardians of our family, in that they knew best how to keep our family together. In their presence, their unconditional love for us never went unfelt.

I was now living with the guilt of my choice, in choosing to stand by my husband instead of meeting my brother during the hour of his greatest need. Perhaps he would have been in a better frame of mind if Joey and I had been there.

I punished myself by not celebrating my birthday for many years, as Quint died the day after my nineteenth birthday.

When I returned to New York I promptly indulged in the fantasy that I'd lost no one. I built an elaborate fantasy life around each of my devastating losses: I'd given birth to Roger's baby and father and son were both well, Mom was still in the hospital fighting her leukemia, and Quint was in South Dakota working the timber in the mountains he loved so much. The pain associated with the grief was so horrific that it would be nearly five years after I lost Mom and Quint that I would even be able to say out loud that they'd died.

24

WENDY LOU TO THE RESCUE

While I thought New York was going to be a new beginning for Logan and me, that wasn't the case. Logan was often away on training expeditions, so Joey and I were alone for the most part. The feeling of isolation and separation from my family only grew. Upon returning home, Logan would shower Joey with an initial spurt of attention but our emotional needs went largely unmet. My husband often came home feeling randy, and my way of telling him I'd missed him was to satisfy him in bed.

In my marriage, I learned that sex was important to Logan, as it is for all men. Men seem to have a built-in animal drive for sex, and I discovered it's deeply validating for a man to witness a woman who he's screwing achieve an orgasm. I learned that one sure-fire way to keep my husband happy was to climax. So, I learned the art of faking the perfect orgasm. I added in plenty of dirty talk and loud moans for good measure.

During the day, I would also think of different ways to enhance our sexual life. I was afraid of him getting bored with me; I needed my husband to need me. Watching porn with my husband, I'd search his expressions to see what he was most excited by. I took note of what physically aroused him. When my husband was turned on by watching lesbians having sex, for instance, I wrote it into my narrative that I'd experimented with women. I made sure I was everything he fantasized about sexually.

Logan was the more social of the two of us. He would try and bring other people into our lives, but I was reluctant to trust anyone. When Logan, Joey, and I finally got our own apartment, I was thrilled.

Though we had our own housing, struggle remained a part of our everyday life. While I hoarded food for Joey, the money would often run out before the end of the month and Logan and I would subsist on the army MREs. I did all of our laundry by hand, including washing Joey's cloth diapers daily. I was a naturally overprotective mother and I never let Joey out of my sight. He slept on my chest nightly and we were never separated for more than a few hours until he was around three years old.

Though I had a family of my own now, I was always homesick for my family back on the farm. I hadn't seen anyone in nearly a year following Quint's funeral so I welcomed my dad when he stopped through New York for a few days on his way down the East Coast.

With Logan hardly able to support our fledgling family on his army stipend, the financial strain put an inordinate amount of pressure on our marriage. Instead of investing in a crib and mattress for Joey, Logan was often self-serving and spent the majority of his income on expensive amplifiers and speakers to feed his music hobby.

Already a compulsive liar, his lies about our dire financial straits were often the source of our worst fights, which were becoming more frequent between us. As time went by, he paid little to no attention to Joey, bordering on the point of neglect, and I started to hate Logan for it.

When the fighting finally stopped, so did the dialogue between us, and we lived like roommates. I could read the writing on the wall and wondered how a marriage could implode so quickly after four years.

Old resentments flared up, namely the infidelity Logan had early on in our relationship just prior to Joey's birth, which I'd never really forgiven him for. When another man named Andrew, who was kind, started to pursue me, I eventually gave in to his advances. The fling was a short affair.

Though I was no longer in Donken, I called Wendy Lou often and she knew all about my hardships with Logan. One day when I'd told her my marriage was on the brink of collapse, Wendy Lou offered to move to upstate New York to help Joey and me get our own place. We were best friends and at an age when we were both young and carefree. I'd just turned twenty.

Once I'd scrapped together enough to get a reliable used car, Joey was always on the go with me. I heard through the grapevine there were some openings at a local restaurant. I started at Fair Grounds bussing dishes, and eventually made more money hosting and waitressing. It was my first job, and I was lucky in that it also brought me an extended family. Everyone always made sure I had enough work to support Joey. With my little man always by my side, he always got plenty of love from everyone. He was a total ham, and a natural performer. He was always the center of attention.

The friendships which were forged at Fair Grounds gave me the support and encouragement to act in the best interest of my son, even if it meant leaving Logan. When I was ready to leave Logan for good, my best friend Wendy Lou was there for me with the additional emotional and moral support I needed. Once Wendy Lou arrived, we promptly got our own place. I was finally able to muster up the courage to leave Logan. Without me anchoring him,

Logan eventually went AWOL and got kicked out of the army.

It was easy for Wendy Lou to join my new family at Fair Grounds. She fit in like a fish in water. We managed to pay the bills on time. We worked all day and, on nights when TJ was with neighborhood friends, we also partied all night. Most important of all, Wendy Lou helped me raise Joey. I couldn't have done it without her. Much to my disappointment, Logan was in and out of Joey's life.

As a toddler, Joey was always getting into mischief. My favorite memory is putting him to bed one night only to have him arise and tiptoe through our living room, unlock our front door, and make his way over to our neighbor's house. As Joey was only three feet tall, his ingenuity prompted him to pull a dining room chair up to the front door in order to unlatch the front lock.

Wendy Lou and I lived in a safe neighborhood and our neighbor Lorne, who was just across the driveway, never locked his front door. To Lorne's surprise that evening, Joey walked in like a happy house guest, plopped on one of the available living room chairs and asked, "What'cha doing?" Lorne gladly provided some milk and cookies for my wayward son.

He was a happy child, who was naturally curious, and was always laughing. We would go exploring on nature walks often. I gave my child every head start I could and enrolled him in a Catholic daycare. I worked day and night to give Joey every material comfort. We celebrated any and every occasion, which laid the foundation for his healthy self-esteem. On this third birthday we celebrated with a big outdoor party; I baked him a Teenage Mutant Ninja Turtle cake, he was obsessed with Leonardo, and I gave him his first boombox as a way to share my love of music with him. He learned all of his spoken vocabulary from KISS songs.

It was a period in my life when I started drinking again.

As it always did, alcohol lowered my social inhibitions and disarmed the painfully self-conscious feelings of being utterly different from other people who I felt relentlessly judged by. I was often the life of the party, which I loved. When I was drinking, I saw myself without blemishes. For a night, I was perfect and I often wondered why I couldn't feel as good sober. Drinking as an adult also helped me cope with the personal demons which had haunted me since high school; alcohol allowed me to rise above the low self-esteem and the self-doubt which riddled me daily.

I'd learned by this point that most men could be controlled by their dicks. Many would do just about anything to satisfy their physical needs, and I loved the power I could wield over the men who pursued me. The sex that went on between Damien and me enslaved me, and I still carried the emotional and mental chains of incest. Needing to break free and exert my own sense of control, I would now decide when to be sexual and with whom.

When a new man caught my eye, I would always see if I could command his attention. Once I did, I would turn him down. It empowered me to know I was in control, not him. I had the power to say no. My self-worth and my sexuality were one and the same; I knew I was good at sex.

However, on the flip side, Damien conditioned me to believe that I was made for sex, which fed into my self-hatred. This falsely held belief distorted how I viewed my sexuality far into my adult years. I would still struggle with this distinction well into mid-life.

Much of the time, I consistently sought out sexual experiences in order to build my self-confidence. But at the same time, I had conflicting feelings of revulsion about my sexual behavior which often led to more shame and guilt. It was an emotional merry-go-round.

However, when the parties started to spill over into my home life, I realized that my drinking life was once again getting out of hand. Seeing Joey surrounded by drinking adults was my wakeup call. It was an echo of my past, in which Damien and I would see our older siblings partying, and I felt guilty about exposing my son prematurely to the more mature aspects of adult life. Those mornings I was hungover, it was hard to get up to take care of Joey. I told Wendy Lou we couldn't party at home anymore, and while I didn't stop drinking, I tried to drink less often.

Logan never paid a dime of child support after the divorce. Even more despicable, however, was that he made no further attempts to see his son. This contradicted everything Logan told me about his love for Joey. Logan always upheld empty promises that he wanted to be a better man and a better father. However, time proved otherwise.

Logan completely disappeared from Joey's life and there was no way to get a hold of him. He seemed to drop off the face of the earth. This made it much easier to decide to move Joey closer to family, and I made immediate plans to move back to the Upper Peninsula. Luckily, my best friend Wendy Lou also agreed to return home to embark on the next chapter of our lives. The best thing I got out of my relationship with Logan was my child. I will always be grateful to him for that.

25

BACK ON THE FARM

At the age of twenty-one, Wendy Lou, Joey and I moved back to Michigan. Dylan and Patty had taken ownership of the farm by this point, and Dad had bought a trailer to put on the farm. He always had a place to stay. With some financial help from my sister Caitlyn, I got my own trailer and also put it on the farm. It was a time in his life when Joey was surrounded by family. My son and I were back in the family fold, and this was a great comfort to me. Wendy Lou and I were both back in the same hometown we'd spent all of our teenage years dreaming about bigger places.

Aunt Jesse, my mom's older sister, was still a part of our family. It was a time when Dad decided he wanted to take over caring for Aunt Jesse. This meant both of them would be on the road together. They made unlikely travel companions, but Aunt Jesse adored my dad and discovered that she loved traveling with him. They had an ease with each other. He was able to make her laugh, and we always believed Dad saw Aunt Jesse as his link to Mom.

When Dad began dating Leah, the young woman who'd cozied up next to him on many an afternoon during my mom's prolonged illness, everyone in the family reviled her. She was a mean-spirited person who drank too much. Later when Leah joined Aunt Jesse and Dad on the road while traveling, she was characteristically unkind to Aunt Jesse who was nothing but lovable.

By the time Damien was heading into his twenties, he'd struggled because he'd failed to cultivate a strong work ethic. He was consistently reliant on the goodwill of his older siblings, especially Dylan, to bail him out of whatever difficult life situation he'd gotten himself into. Damien suffered from a defeated mindset, in which he felt the world was against him and he could never catch a lucky break. After a while, he would marinate himself in his self-conceived notion of "poor me."

In the years after I'd given birth to Joey, our adult lives had taken Damien and me to different places. Damien now had three children of his own. He and his new girlfriend Emily were raising their family on the farm as well, in their own trailer. It was our own village. The O'Brien Village. I'd hoped fatherhood would keep Damien on the straight and narrow. Time would eventually prove otherwise. Little did I know that my betrayal blindness was still in full force allowing me to relate to Damien as a brother. I remembered none of the abuse until the age of twenty-six.

Putting my memories in a locked room worked, although my amnesia wasn't airtight. While I'd repressed everything so thoroughly during my waking hours, night terrors were a constant part of my life. My ongoing nightmares didn't spare me any details; I felt the tactile heaviness of my abuser on top of me, so much so that I couldn't breathe. Instead of a penis penetrating me, I felt as if a sharp instrument was piercing my vagina, stabbing me. Even my sense of smell was heightened while dreaming. His breath reeked of the smell of semen.

Eventually, the terrors which I experienced in my

nightmares began to leak their way into my waking hours. It was all so puzzling. I kept seeing flashes of a monster with a green, elongated, face with red eyes. Always the red eyes. Though I told no one, the name I gave this monster was simply *"Him"*. It got me thinking that perhaps in an act of self-defense, I'd stabbed *"Him"* or committed something equally drastic. There was no other rational explanation I could think of for all the many memories that were just…gone.

I didn't notice how much of my childhood I couldn't remember, until people close to me would bring up shared experiences. They often dismissed it as a casual memory lapse with the words, "Everyone forgets stuff." Other times, I would sheepishly pretend that I recalled something I didn't. When this happened frequently enough, I realized and began to accept that my mind was most likely masking something I either survived or something I did. Though, it was up in the air which one.

When talking about my childhood with anyone, I felt like my fragmented memories were unreal and distant. The memories I *did* have were foggy. This bothered me so much. The thoughts that I'd hurt someone became crippling. Soon, there was no part of me that was beyond the pain of carrying an enormous guilt complex.

Damien and I, finding that we were both back on the farm at the same time, were spending a rare moment together alone. We were in my trailer listening to good music and playing cards. Damien and I were recalling our family's stories and how great Quint and Mom were. It had been five years since both had passed away, and I was finally able to accept that they were no longer around. In the years since, I could never open up about my loss until now.

Both Damien and I were pretty buzzed and I was very emotional by this point. I started revealing how bothered I was by such huge gaps in my memory. I found myself confiding in him about my guilt; I always assumed that whatever had happened that I couldn't recollect, I was the guilty party. I was almost certain that I was the aggressor rather than the aggrieved.[7]

I said, "You were around me the most when we were growing up. Do you think I could have done something that horrible?" I figured, if I had, he would have been my only witness. Maybe he knew something I didn't.

He said, "Ya, probably something did happen. I could see you doing something like that." Hearing this from him troubled me. The only times I could remember clearly were happy times spent with Roger and Wendy Lou, and our large family gatherings. "It's funny, I don't remember a lot of the times you and I were messing around here on the farm," I said casually.

My words landed with an impact I hadn't expected, and the briefest expression of both surprise and fear crossed his face, which he immediately replaced with a vacant stare. The faintest, shrill, sound of an alarm rang inside of me. Damien then said something that has always stayed in my mind. He said, "Ya, we *all* messed around together; we were just kids." He was minimizing the impact of what he'd done and could not now undo. He was justifying his past actions to himself, and covering his tracks. It would be five years before I found out the truth.

26

MY SELF-WORTH

With both of us back in our hometown, Wendy Lou and I got a job working at the same bar, Jake's Bar, and that made it easy to continue to party as we had in New York. We partied with guys that would come into the bar, some of whom were tourists from out of state. They would buy us drinks all night long and after we'd close down the bar, we'd continue to party. My mind could rest easy because Joey was well taken care of at the farm with Patty, and I would pick him up the next morning.

The male attention I got continued throughout my twenties and thirties, and I continued to enjoy flirting with men. I hardly ever slept with any of the guys I would flirt with and can count on one hand the number of men who I've actually had intercourse with on one hand. The few times when I'd have a casual encounter, I never had an orgasm. I would learn in future relationships that when I was physically intimate, I would need to condition myself to stay in the present moment in order to enjoy the experience. My satisfaction came from knowing I could please who I was with.

Patty once said of me, "You *ooze* sexuality." It was something men could smell a mile away and I made it known to them, whether it was true or not, that I could fulfill their fantasies in unorthodox ways. More than the act of intercourse itself, I discovered the true aphrodisiac was in making the man I'm seducing believe I wanted him sexually. In the same way that I could make myself look older than I was, I could also communicate I was more sexually experienced than I really was.

I kept up this ruse up over the years and Patty and Caitlyn always thought I was hyper-sexual and always assumed that I loved having sex and was having lots of it. I was so convincing at keeping up the charade that both of them shared this opinion for many years. In part, it made me feel normal to be seen as sex positive, and it aligned with the outgoing persona I embodied while I was drinking.

In reality, because I was so used to dissociating with Damien, I was detached from any pleasure I might have derived during the actual act of penetration and intercourse. Often, I was too busy faking my enjoyment. Completely numb in my nether regions, as a survivor of incest, I felt it was my job to please. My entire self-worth was wrapped up in this idea. It never occurred to me to be more attuned to what I might need.

27

AN OLDER MAN

When I met my second husband, I was doing what I considered to be really well for myself. Logan, Joey's dad, was out of the picture by then and I wasn't receiving any child support. My job at Jake's bar was keeping my household afloat. While I felt guilty about needing to go back to work with Joey being so young, it was a necessity. I knew Joey was in good hands with his Aunt Patty.

One night while I was at work, a devastatingly beautiful, older, man who was a dead ringer for Mel Gibson walked in. When he looked at me, I felt like I was the only woman in the room. Once he had my full attention, he confidently approached the bar and, taking a seat, wasted no time in introducing himself with a simple, "Hi, I'm Luke."

I couldn't suppress my smile and appreciated how matter of fact he was. As I was about to tell him my name, he said, "I know who you are." He told me that he went to school with my siblings Dylan, Caitlyn, and Quint.

When I learned I'd also gone to school with his younger siblings Joni and Mia, it put me at ease. Around here, everyone knew everyone and after that initial night, Luke started coming in to visit me more often.

He was about twelve years my senior and compared to my first husband Logan, who couldn't hold down a job to save his life, Luke seemed to have his act together. Once I knew he was interested in getting to know me better, I told him I had a son. Luke seemed thrilled that I had a boy.

My initial impression of Luke was that I'd found someone to talk to who wouldn't judge me for my past mistakes and who genuinely seemed to care for me. Even though I grew up in a tight-knit family, I always felt like I needed to do everything on my own, and it was nice after meeting Luke to feel taken care of for the first time in my life.

Once we got to talking, we were inseparable and we talked about what seemed like everything. We discussed the town we grew up in and the small town values we shared. He was an avid listener and wanted to hear all about my past.

When he looked at me with his stunning green eyes and said, "The first time I saw you laughing, I'd never seen anyone as beautiful as you," a shiver ran down my spine. Later he would tell me that meeting me was, for him at least, love at first sight.

Had I finally met someone who could really love me unconditionally, and did I deserve to be loved like that? Growing up, there were countless times when I felt dirty, ugly, and scared.

My siblings Caitlyn and Dylan, who'd gone to school with him, tried to warn me to stay away from Luke because he had a horrible reputation as a womanizer, a drug user, and a control freak. But that was back then, I told myself. This was now. I tried to assure my concerned family that he would be different with me. Their portrayal of him was nothing like the charming man I'd met and gotten to know in recent days. When I confronted him about my family's warnings, he vowed that he had changed. I threw caution to the wind, and I chose to believe him.

Luke didn't need very long to figure me out. He sensed right away that my whole world revolved around my son Joey, and Luke kept asking to meet him. I had my reservations at first and didn't want to introduce Joey to a man who might not be a permanent fixture in our lives, but soon, I relented.

One night when we were all eating out together, Joey climbed into Luke's lap. When I saw Joey's adoration for Luke, my heart just melted. Luke looked me in the eyes and said, "I want to be his father. I want for us to be a family." I saw, for a brief glimpse, which I could only hope would be true. How nice it would be for Joey to have a stable father figure in his life. And maybe I would finally get the family life I've always wanted.

Though the mutual attraction between us was strong, we made it a point to get to know each other before jumping into bed together. Sex had never been a true source of pleasure for me, and often times sex was just something I needed to endure and get done with in order to please my partner.

The first time Luke and I made love, it was a scene right out of the movies. He was gentle when he touched me and generous with his affection. Maybe because I trusted him, I let myself feel pleasure, which was very uncharacteristic of me.

Luke's touch was incredibly passionate and differed from the innocence and tenderness I shared with Roger. When I experienced my first orgasm with Luke, it cast a spell over me and I looked at him and said, "I knew you were *The One*." Then, without missing a beat, he said, "I've waited forever for you." Both of us caught up in the beauty of the moment, when Luke whispered in my ear, "Will you marry me?" I whispered back, "Yes."

28

EARLY WARNING SIGNS

C aitlyn, who never trusted him, said that Luke seemed to want to track my every move. I brushed off her early warning signs and told her it was Luke's way of expressing love for me. One time, on a planned vacation to South Carolina with Caitlyn, Luke called non-stop telling me that he missed me. When he asked me what I was doing and with whom, I again interpreted it as him taking a friendly interest. While he didn't accuse me of meeting other men at that point, his inquiries left me feeling like I had to defend myself, though I'd done nothing wrong.

It's only after we'd been together for a while that I began to notice Luke's controlling behavior, particularly his intense streaks of jealousy, which became more pronounced as time between us passed. I noticed how insecure Luke got whenever I craved time away from him to spend time with family and friends. Though Luke had his own circle of family and friends, I observed how emotionally dependent he was on me.

One day in June, a month before our wedding, I got a true sense of his darker side which terrified me. Patty had agreed to watch Joey, and Luke and I planned a carefree day of bar-hopping from Donken to Ontonagon.

Arriving at an old dive with a wooden bar, I'd noticed a stranger's initials carved into the wood. It got me thinking of my amiable nephew Andrew and I made a passing remark saying, "I know an Andrew." By that point, Luke had met most of my family, but not all of my extended family, which was quite large.

In a sudden rage, Luke stood up and barked at me, "Let's go." Getting into the car I distinctly remember feeling hyper-nervous around him. I told myself I must have done something wrong but didn't know what. He was speeding down the long road we were driving on, but said nothing else until I finally broke the silence and asked what was upsetting him.

With a maniacal look in his eyes that I remember as pure evil, he said, "I will not put up with you daydreaming about the guy you had an affair with. I know his name was Andrew, and you were caressing his name on that bar top, thinking of him."

I sat there stunned by the misunderstanding. It's true that I'd cheated on my first husband with a guy named Andrew but it was by pure coincidence that he shared my nephew's name. The one infidelity I'd regrettably had while still married to Logan was a distant memory to me. Did I really look wistfully at the carved initials in the bar? Was I actually thinking about Andrew the guy I had a casual fling with? The self-doubt crept in followed by self-blame.

I wanted to speak up and clear the air but something about Luke's facial expression was so graphic to me that it gave me the creeps. I suddenly felt incredibly vulnerable around a man whose most charismatic quality to me was his ability to protect me. I suddenly felt like a piece of shit, like I was somehow deserving of this awful turn of events.

Driving at speeds of up to ninety miles an hour, I

begged him to slow the car down. When he finally screeched to a halt, he got out of the car and walked around to my side. I thought he was going to ask me to walk the rest of the way home. Instead, aggressively throwing the door open, he grabbed my hair and dragged me out of the car. I was stunned and said, "I'm sorry! I'm so sorry!" over and over again.

This seemed to embolden him and he yelled, "You wanna be a slut?" He continued screaming inches away from my face, "Do you want to be a whore? Do you want to act like a whore?" By this point I was crying, but Luke was unfazed. Continuing to manhandle me, he pushed my face towards his crotch. "Then suck this," he said.

His words left me ashamed, humiliated, degraded, and feeling worthless. These were familiar feelings to me. It's only later that I would realize that I was acting out a script for how survivors react in violent situations like this one.[8]

We were still twenty miles from Donken. When we got back into the car, I couldn't look at him and turned my head away looking out the passenger window. It was not a quiet ride back home, in fact, Luke's verbal insults and personal attacks continued until we were approaching the outskirts of town.

It's only when we got closer to the farm that his demeanor changed. Rationalizing his unacceptable behavior by saying that I should have known better than to say what I did, he was now in a last-ditch effort to save face. By abandoning any responsibility for his offenses, he was now shifting the blame onto me. Later in my marriage, I would learn this was textbook behavior for an abuser.

When he observed that I was still in a messy, teary, state he rolled the car to another full stop before we reached the farm so I could clean up my smeared makeup. As I looked into the mirror, my bloodshot eyes stared back at me. My survival instincts took over and I heard an inner voice telling me to _RUN_.

I defensively elbowed Luke in the ribs and then I leapt out of the car. Once on my feet, I ran as fast as my legs would carry me through the woods I knew so well, trying to put as much distance between us as possible.

Eventually making it all the way home to the farm, I ran up to our front door. I looked and felt like a wreck. Both Dylan and Damien were shocked to see the state I was in. My oldest brother Dylan offered me no comfort and reminded me that all the wedding invitations had already been sent out. It was too late to back out of the wedding plans now. Then, very insensitively, he added, "You knew what you were in for when you started seeing Luke."

Damien, who was already half in the can, suggested we go to a bar and get drunk. We ended up at a spot called Uphill, which had a dance floor. I started drinking, and then he said something that sounded eerily familiar to me though I couldn't pinpoint why. "Let's play a game," he said with ease. Something about the words triggered me, and I saw a quick flash of a monster, still unidentified to me. Was he trying to reframe his sexual abuse as something I would possibly think back on as a special time in our lives?

Then he said the strangest thing. "I'm going to pretend I'm gay. It will be fun to see other people's reactions," he said. Once he'd gotten me onto the dance floor, under the pretense of being gay, he gave himself license to touch my body all over again in a hyper-sexual way. While I was inebriated, I knew that I was uncomfortable and growing more so by the minute. He seemed to quickly forget about the evening in the days that followed and life went on. We never talked about it, and it would be another four years before I recalled everything that transpired between us.

In the years following, Damien and I would continue to see each other when the family got together. I started feeling strangely uncomfortable around him after the fiasco on the dance floor. I no longer trusted him but still had no concrete reason to justify what my distrust stemmed from.

Damien's other character flaws became more apparent to me, as I started seeing him for who he really was. I was fed up that he never seemed to grow up. He still put on an act of being a helpless lost little boy, and my patience for his antics was wearing thin.

He could never hold down a job to support his kids. They were on welfare and had to accept handouts wherever they could. Patty and Dylan supplied food, money, and even transportation. Damien never learned that there's a consequence for every action. Always self-indulgent, as he got older, he also became more self-absorbed. Damien drank heavily and developed a bad drug habit. He looked like a bum, and lived like one.

IT'LL NEVER HAPPEN AGAIN

Following Luke's violent outburst, he showed up at the farm asking for me. He wanted to talk and was very apologetic; with his red eyes, it was obvious he'd been crying. Coming to me looking so defeated and tortured, I was conflicted. I felt both anger and empathy at the same time.

Apologizing, he blamed his behavior on the alcohol and he made sure to tell me he loved me. "That wasn't me, it was the alcohol. Yes, I was jealous but can you blame me? You *did* have an affair with a guy named Andrew." I conceded nothing, and wished I hadn't trusted him so much with details about my first marriage.

I stood my ground, at least for a little while, and told him the wedding was off and that I wouldn't marry him. He told me that it would be a massive disappointment for both of our families to cancel the wedding now. Then he proceeded to lie to us both by saying, "It'll never happen again."

I thought about Joey's welfare. Luke wanted to adopt Joey and always told me while we were dating that Joey needed a father. While my family wasn't thrilled by the initial news of our engagement, over time both of our families had come around. My Dad always liked Luke, and they had a good rapport. I think my Dad related so well to Luke because he saw a reflection of his younger self in Luke.

I found many similarities between both men. Superficially, both were naturally charming. On a deeper level of comparison, I discovered both of them were victims of sexual abuse by women in their youth. While my father endured ongoing sexual abuse by his stepmother Vivian, Luke was also abused by a female baby-sister who would fondle his genitals and make fun of the size and shape of his genitalia. This would never have been disclosed or discussed openly between the two men. I believe neither man understood the correlating link between their insecurities and their history of sexual abuse.[9]

Seeing both men through the lens of abuse, I better understood their shared traits of hyper-masculinity and their need, as adults, to dominate and control me and others. The once popular idea that the earlier a boy is introduced to the world of sex, the sooner he becomes a man is preposterous. This misnomer frames abuse in the context of "getting lucky".

The problems that emerge include confusion at the time the abuse is taking place, followed by lifelong problems with intimacy from a fractured emotional security. The men remain terribly insecure, and without proper counseling, this results in an inability to trust a romantic significant other. When sex does take place with a female partner a man claims to love, it's about domination and control.

30

BABY EVAN

I walked down the aisle and married Luke. Everyone showed up to support me. My dad had on his best suit, and he gave me away. Joey was the ring bearer. My young nieces were the flower girls. We marked the day as a happy occasion, and I wished Quint and Mom could've both been there. I couldn't have known that I was embarking on a marriage very much like the one my mom had with my dad.

Newly married, I wanted to make my relationship with Luke work. Being a single parent working nonstop to support Joey, our life had been full of challenges. Luke had a good job in Superior, WI, four hours away, and that's where we settled. I was grateful that Joey had two parents again, and that we would be a family. Luke had a fun-loving and carefree side to his personality and could often be both generous and kind. This was always in stark contrast to his much darker side.

When things were good with Luke, things were *really* good. Especially the sex. Luke was very passionate, and there was always lots of passionate kissing. The way he looked at me and held an intense gaze communicated to me when he found me sexy. I loved his firm touch. He would literally sweep me off my feet. Picking me up, I would wrap my legs around his waist and we often had sex all over the house. I loved the way he would run his fingers through my hair, tugging at it in a way that heightened my arousal.

Often times the passion was so hot that we'd be having sex before we even got our clothes off. He was well endowed, and I initiated sex often. If my husband got off on having rough sex, I acted like I loved it hard and fast. My philosophy was Anything Goes.

We couldn't really get enough of each other physically and our mutual attraction to each other endured over the life of the whole marriage. Our robust sex life was one of the main reasons I stayed in my marriage too long. He gave me a million reasons to leave him, but sex was not one of them. In fact, after major arguments, or periods of separation, we always made up with sex.

Emotionally, our relationship was on a collision course as we became more dependent on each other as the years went on. Our feelings would intensify, but we rarely knew how to handle such strong emotions.

Starting our new life together in Superior, WI, everything seemed okay, at first. Luke had old-fashioned values and clear-cut roles for men and women. So I made Luke a full course breakfast every morning and packed his lunch too. Then I got Joey off to preschool each day before I would head to my job at the local credit union where I was working as a teller.

A few months into our marriage, Luke started showing up at my workplace. Then Luke began to drop comments about my work attire. Nothing he initially said was too alarming, and I made nothing of it, but things became eerie for me very quickly when he started showing up at my workplace more frequently.

I would look up surprised to see him standing in my line,

as I registered the same dreaded feeling of fear I'd tried to shelve in the few days preceding our wedding day. I soon realized I was afraid of my husband. While he always feigned his visits as casual drop-ins, his possessiveness was thinly veiled. I always felt as if Luke's intention was to catch me in the act of doing something wrong.

Perhaps Luke could sense my fear, which might have made him more bold. He began to abuse me verbally. He wasn't throwing punches yet, but he would call me names that wounded my pride. He would call me a slut, when he thought I was acting like one. Joey, while still young, could understand Luke's words and the terrified look on Joey's face broke my heart. I would scoop my son up in my arms and try to get away from Luke as quickly as possible by leaving the room, but wherever we went in the house Luke followed.

These verbal tirades were not fueled by alcohol much of the time. So I came to realize and sadly accept that this was just the way Luke was when he flew off the handle. Not only did his workplace visits rattle me, but he started following me wherever I went. If I said I was going to the grocery store, he needed to follow me there to make sure I wasn't lying. I began to feel consistently unsafe in his presence and, as a result, I felt really unhinged.

The first few months of our marriage were a series of highs and lows, a pattern that would repeat throughout the entirety of our relationship. After growing up in a dysfunctional home where I had to keep secrets my whole life, I had plenty of practice burying my emotions. I dealt with my fears the only way I know how; I forced myself to focus on Luke's better qualities, of which there were many, in order to survive the lows. When he wanted to be, he could be downright charming. I sometimes felt like I married my father.

Our good days really did feel like newlywed bliss.

Eventually, Luke convinced me to go off the pill. I

wanted another child, and I thought it would make Luke feel more secure in our marriage. Within a month, I was pregnant and I was genuinely ecstatic at the thought of bringing new life into the world. Joey, who Luke adopted not long after the wedding, was six at the time. When I told Luke I was carrying his child, he was elated. In the days following, he treated me like royalty and I didn't have to lift a finger.

Sad to say, after unforeseen circumstances forced Luke's sister Joni and her boyfriend Mark to temporarily move in with us, Luke's insecurities were back on the rise with the presence of another man in the house. He would make the most far-flung accusations, at one point accusing me of having sexual feelings for Mark. It broke my heart that we were back at square one again. I was bewildered.

At a four-month, prenatal, check-up, Luke and I got to listen to our baby's heartbeat. When we returned home following the appointment, Luke accused Mark and me of foul play. In his jealous rage, he shoved my back against a door, entrapping me. I remember feeling so distressed that I felt like I couldn't take it anymore. My body was in a state of high stress, and I was nearly hysterical.

Then the following week at my ultrasound appointment, things got very quiet in the room, and my doctor was notified. When she examined me she confirmed, "There's no heartbeat." *Not again*, I thought to myself. I couldn't believe what I was hearing; the same dire words I'd heard years before on the day I delivered my son Joey by caesarean. I demanded a second opinion at a different hospital; they concurred that we'd lost our baby.

A few days later, I was induced and experienced all the labor pains of delivering a healthy child. The contractions were horrible. Finally, I had to push. They cut the umbilical cord of my stillborn child and Luke and my sister Caitlyn got to hold his tiny body before they took him away to perform an autopsy. His birth and death certificate are the same date.

We found out our baby had a stroke in utero. I found myself blaming Luke, and before long those feelings of blame morphed into hate. I also blamed myself, for making the wrong choice again, and for being stuck in another unhappy marriage.

My body was in rebellion; two days later I was back in the hospital hemorrhaging badly. My doctor chose to dilate my cervix and surgically scraped out my uterine lining in order to prevent infection and additional bleeding. The child I'd been carrying came into this world not breathing, its lifeless body a small gray mass. While he was no longer in my womb during my subsequent surgery, I believed I heard a baby crying for me and wondered in the far outskirts of my mind if he was still alive though the results of autopsy were in by then. I named the baby I lost Evan, after my father's middle name.

31

CHANGING BEFORE MY EYES

The physical abuse in my marriage got worse following our personal tragedy. I felt isolated from my best friend Wendy Lou, who was busy living her own life in New Hampshire. Luke deterred me from establishing close friendships with anyone in town, and without my family close by to confide in, I kept most of the abuse I endured to myself.

One of the side effects of my long-term sexual abuse was to put an inordinate amount of pressure on myself to live up to expectations in the different roles in my life. Instead of admitting to the emotional and physical abuse happening in my struggling second marriage, I wanted to be somebody else. Tired of feeling like a victim, I wanted to be someone capable who had it all together. A superwoman. I didn't want my family to pity me, so I kept my struggles hidden.

And as a mother, I always felt Joey was mine, and not either of his dads'. During the periods of our life when it was just Joey and me, I was always determined to fill the role of both parents. With the volatile dynamics in my marriage to Luke, I could see the ways in which my son was being adversely affected. Every time Luke and I would fight, I felt like we were chipping away at the joyful innocence that had once been the hallmark of Joey's happy childhood.

Joey kept all his emotions inside; my son, who was always a happy-go-lucky child, like I was in the years before my own abuse, was changing before my eyes. I would try and talk with him about his feelings, but he always said he was *fine*. It was as if he was learning to tamp down all of his unpleasant emotions in the same way I often did to cope with the stresses in my life.

Over the years, I'd done a very effective job of portraying myself as someone with a strong sense of self. I mimicked traits I saw in my sister Caitlyn and Dad, particularly their strength, and modeled myself after them. In some ways, later in life, I'd draw on this strength to help me through my most difficult transitions.

There was a lot of pretending at that point in my marriage. I remember one time we were en route to Luke's parents' home and he began lashing out again, as he was so prone to doing. His accusations always seemed to come out of thin air and he would stay enraged. When we arrived at his parents', however, we would act as if everything was okay between us.

His parents had taken to me and embraced me as their daughter-in-law when Luke and I first got together. They were thrilled that Luke had finally found someone who could ground him, and marveled at how changed their son seemed at the beginning of our marriage. I felt a strong expectation to keep up appearances even as things were falling apart. This contradiction and the denial of the ongoing mental abuse and the escalating physical violence that really took place was incredibly confusing for Joey, who witnessed all of it.

Luke also took incremental steps to isolate me more from my family each year that passed. My in-laws were only six miles from my family's farm. Whenever we went back to visit his family, Luke would always come up with reasons as to why we couldn't drop by the farm.

There was a Jekyll and Hyde[10a] quality about Luke; a conversation with him could turn on a dime. Over the years, I got better at reading Luke, and could see when the switch would flip. The physical transformation that took place in him as he was stewing over one of his many insecurities was startling: his eyes would get squinty, his jaw line would harden, and his body would become tense and rigid; these physical signs would alert me to something big coming.

One time during another one of Luke's jealous rages, I couldn't handle anymore of his accusations that evening and tried to remove myself from the toxic situation in the hopes that he would calm down on his own. Not wanting to sleep in the same bed with him that night, I sought refuge in my son's bedroom and was snuggling with Joey as he slept. Luke was relentless and he didn't know when to quit.

Joey woke up to sounds of Luke choking me, and seeing me struggle, my son immediately broke into tears screaming, "Stop, Daddy, stop!" I thought I was a goner. When Luke stopped, just short of me passing out, he donned the strangest expression on his face, almost as if he didn't know what possessed him to do such a thing. He was becoming incredibly dangerous, and my ability to shield my then six-year-old son from the harsh reality of Luke's abusive behavior was diminishing.

If I alluded in any way to his emotional instability by saying something like, "There's something wrong with you" or "You're acting psycho", that would push him over the edge. He always wore a façade of normalcy and, admittedly, he tried so hard to be normal. The fact that he might need some help with his mental health was a primary threat to his masculinity. Things would come to blows after that. While some days I knew it was in my best interest to let him have the upper hand, most days I was a fighter and I defended myself with all that I had.

Another one of Luke's major insecurities was me leaving him. If I were to say, "I'm done with this" or "I'm not gonna put up with this anymore", he'd lash out verbally and sometimes physically, grabbing and shaking me. He'd actively take steps to isolate me, often taking away the phone and car keys. He'd also leave me stranded in the house, unable to go to work.

When Luke was in the privacy of our own home, he had no inhibitions. After a physical altercation, when I'd flee to another part of the house, Luke would trail me into a closed room. I'd scream at him, "I need to be alone," but he wouldn't leave me be. He gave me zero personal space, which was beyond suffocating.

One of the most violent encounters was when Luke pulled a gun on me. I learned years later from Joey that Luke claimed he was often on drugs which clouded his judgment and amplified his anger. While Luke has apologized for his actions since, I'll never forget the terror of that evening.

We had gone out earlier in the evening, and we had both done a fair amount of drinking. Luke, as he typically did, became threatened when another man began talking to me. While he always had to keep his cool in public, he would unleash all of his misdirected wrath when we got home. The more I would deny his ridiculous accusations, the angrier he would get.

Scared of his uncontrollable rage, my gut instinct told me to get out of the house. After tackling me to the ground that night, I found myself staring down the barrel of a gun, with my husband's finger on the trigger. That night Luke's sister called and could surmise from the shaky tone of my voice that something was terribly wrong. She had the good sense to call the police. Once the police arrived, Luke went quietly into their custody.

The day after the arrest, I gathered all of my personal possessions, and Joey and I fled to St. Ignace, Michigan to stay with Caitlyn until I could figure out my next move.

32

NOT MY BABY

With Caitlyn's help I rented a house, got a new job managing a motel, and Joey and I were doing well again. Things calmed down considerably, and I hated myself for the way I would still recall the good times I'd shared with Luke, despite his awful abuse which had gotten so out of control.

Then, Joey broke his arm at the age of seven. As an overprotective mom, I was hysterical seeing my son in such pain. Joey started asking for Luke, who Joey was calling Dad by then. Luke drove the ten hours to be with him that very night and he begged me to have another chance at our family; Luke said Joey needed a dad. He said he'd gotten help for his rage, and that he was now going to anger management classes. I chose to believe him because that's what I wanted to hear.

It had been three months since we separated and I was terribly lonely. The memory of his awful behavior had already started to fade, and before I knew it, we ended up in bed together again.

Because I'd gone off the pill after our separation, I told Luke I didn't want him to come inside of me, but when he should have pulled out, he held me down and finished inside me. Then he said, "Now you can't leave me, because I just got you pregnant."

As fate would have it, I *did* conceive that night, our second child Noah. After I learned I was pregnant, I decided to not give up on my marriage to Luke just yet. I told myself, as I always did, maybe things would be different this time around.

After Joey and I rejoined Luke in Superior, things were blissful for a while as I became more excited at the prospect of having another baby. I loved being pregnant because, after giving birth to Joey, I knew that my children would grow up to be my pride and joy.

Luke and I were fine, until we weren't. His jealousy and insecure rage were displayed in full force again one evening when he got too drunk. In retrospect, he was also probably under the influence of drugs. He was fine earlier in the day, but sometime throughout the day, someone must have planted imaginary doubts in his head.

Perhaps someone who had plans to create a wedge in my marriage. Easily swayed because of his shaky sense of self, he was an easy target for believing these kinds of insinuations. He was convinced that the child we'd recently conceived together wasn't his baby.

The switch had flipped. It was Jekyll and Hyde all over again. He called me every name in the book, as he had in the past, and told me my due date was wrong. He yelled, "Who did you fuck? That's not my baby."

It was the middle of the night when he demanded that I leave our house; the home I'd returned to only recently after he'd convinced me that he had changed. He grabbed my possessions, as well as Joey's things, and threw them down the stairs as if he was disposing of all we owned.

I collected Joey and it took every fiber of resolve I had within me to say to my son, "we are going on an adventure."

It broke my heart to do this to him again. I called my dad to come pick me up and I moved back to St. Ignace where I stayed with Caitlyn while I was unemployed and pregnant.

I fell into a deep depression where I would stay in bed all day and cry. Everything traumatic that I had endured throughout my marriage to Luke came to a head, and my mental health became very fragile. I couldn't properly take care of my son; luckily Caitlyn was there to step in and watch Joey for me.

The idea of being on my own again was incredibly depressing. While pregnant, I had no money, and no place to live except for Caitlyn's exceptional generosity. I was working part-time but it wasn't even enough to cover my and Joey's basic needs, let alone prepare for a new baby.

Throughout this second separation, Luke would call from time to time to check on my welfare and it would bring on a new wave of confusion and depression. I learned to hate him all over again.

During my stay with Caitlyn, I continued to go to my doctor's appointments. I asked the doctor during a routine ultrasound appointment to pinpoint the date of conception. Luke needed proof that the baby was his. When Luke saw the picture of his baby, he had a change of heart and began pleading with me to give our family another chance.

Sadly, during this time of separation in which things were up in the air between us, Luke was seduced by his boss at work and ended up sleeping with her. I'd heard through the grapevine months before that she'd had her sights on my husband for a while. The infidelity came at a time when Luke needed a boost in his bruised ego. Unfortunately, I didn't find out about the infidelity until after Luke had convinced me to move back.

I truly hated this tug of war between us in which we'd repair our relationship only to have things crumble again. I always had to reconvince myself of what Luke reassured me

of each time he'd beg me to return: *it'll be different this time.*
After I moved back again, it was a peaceful period before I
found out about his affair. When I confronted him, he
admitted to it. In light of everything I'd endured as a result
of his jealous insecurities, I felt this was the worst thing he
could ever have put me through. I felt a deeper resentment
for him than I'd ever felt before.

Three months later, Noah arrived. He was a beautiful
baby boy. Noah looked just like Luke and I felt my broken
heart begin to heal as I was holding our baby in my arms.
Luke bonded with Noah right away and was ecstatic to have
another son. Throughout the time that I was nursing, I
moved into the spare bedroom downstairs so my husband
wouldn't be awoken so often during the middle of the night.

I had newfound feelings of peace and hope for the
future that helped to restore the broken parts of me. Joey
would come down in the mornings and we'd all snuggle
together before school. He was in awe of his little brother. It
was a beautiful time for me; my heart was full.

33

ON THE HILL

When Noah was just a couple months old, Luke had an injury on the job in which he'd sliced off a part of his finger. He couldn't work in the interim while he healed so we all decided to enjoy a long vacation together in the hills of Michigan. We camped out in an area where we ultimately wanted to build a family cabin. It was land that we already owned and we frequented it as much as possible; we went there so much we'd call it 'The Hill'.

We took an extended vacation of three months away from everything, and it was a very calm and stable time in our marriage. We'd brought the kids with us, and we didn't have a care in the world.

I loved being in the woods, the four of us together. Luke and I had a chance to talk openly with each other in a way we hadn't for years. Whatever offenses there were in the marriage, he was always able to sweep me off my feet and I always found it in my heart to forgive him. I let go of the anger of feeling betrayed, when I saw him make great strides in being both a nurturing father and attentive spouse.

While the mental abuse and the physical intimidation

could be acute, it wasn't all the time. Our sex life had taken a backseat for a while but on The Hill, Luke and I rekindled our passion. On a very romantic night under the stars, I asked Luke to come lay with me by the fire and I got pregnant with our daughter. When we found out, Luke was happy about the news; on one hand, it gave him another chance to renew his commitment as a father to our children, while on the other hand, he seemed to relish that I would be even more dependent on him.

While I was pregnant, it was a sigh of relief that Luke wasn't prone to his jealous rages. Luke's jealously often stemmed from his fear of abandonment that I would leave him for someone else. I think he felt secure because I'd gained a lot of weight by then, and now carrying my third child.

The arrival of our little princess, a beautiful baby girl we named Nichole, marked such a happy occasion for me that I felt my world was complete; I now had a daughter. I'd hoped for a baby girl while pregnant and I dreamed that we would be close. When she arrived, I wept tears of joy. I remember looking down at Nichole's perfect face; I couldn't believe that I could be so blessed.

34

THE MORE THE MERRIER

Nichole's birth ushered in a period of calm and happiness in the marriage, but just as I was beginning to relax and enjoy my family life, the rug would be pulled out from under my feet.

Now that we had more kids, we moved into a larger home in a new neighborhood. The house was spacious. With my many experiences babysitting growing up, I looked for opportunities to work out of the comfort of my home so that I could keep an eye on my kids while still contributing to our household.

I hired a young babysitter named Karen who was always willing to watch Noah and Nichole while they were young. Karen became a trusted family friend, and pretty soon introduced me to Kyra, who would become my new best friend. Kyra lived just two houses down from us, and after she noticed how good I was with her kids, she introduced me to other parents who needed daycare as well. Soon, my daycare business was up and running.

When Aunt Jesse's health began to fail, in her seventies, she became permanently wheelchair bound, and needed to stop traveling with my dad. Luke and I took over responsibilities from my dad to become her primary caretaker. Aunt Jesse needed to be constantly watched while eating, because she was prone to choking. Eventually, I couldn't keep up with the amount of care that was required and I took steps to enroll her in adult daycare while I was working.

Joey was such a great nephew to his Aunt Jesse. We had a bathroom upstairs and he assisted her in climbing the steps up to the second floor where the bathroom was. He was only twelve at the time, but he seemed to take pride in being able to assist his aunt in this way. Once she started adult day care, Joey selflessly walked the four blocks during the hottest summer days to pick her up and to roll Aunt Jesse back while she was seated in her wheelchair. He always addressed her respectfully as 'Aunt Jesse', and sang her favorite hillbilly songs on request.

While she was living with us Aunt Jesse would become an innocent bystander, a witness to all the manic ups and downs between Luke and I. She would always get worked up during our fights and would ask me afterwards if I was okay. I always assured her, everything was *fine*. As her health continued to decline, Caitlyn and Patty convinced me that it was time for Aunt Jesse to have around the clock care.

We moved her back to Michigan to a nursing home close to Patty. This was one of the harder decisions I had to make in my life. Aunt Jesse was family, and I staunchly believed that you always take care of your own. As my mom's sister, she was a fixture in my life for as long as I'd known my mother. I was overcome with a sense of guilt when I had to admit to myself that I could no longer care for her at the level of meeting her many increasing needs.

35

LUKE TO A TEE

As with all vicious cycles of abuse[10b], the blissful period between Luke and I never lasted for long. As soon as I started doing well with my own business, trouble was on the way. Getting my own revenue stream enabled me to feel more independent from Luke. While I didn't throw this in Luke's face, I could perceive a build-up of tension in my spouse who began to view the extra money I made as a threat.

Then, as Kyra and I became closer as friends and spent more time together, Luke would start in with snarky verbal comments meant to undercut me and my friendship. He was threatened by Kyra from day one, because she was a single, strong, and independent woman. The less time I spent with her the better, lest I begin to desire her independence. As all abusers do, he was strategically isolating me.

By that point, I'd gotten so sick of his bullshit that whatever illusions I'd had about him or our marriage fell away likes scales from my eyes. Of course, he blamed me for letting Kyra come between us in our marriage, claiming that I was prioritizing a friendship with Kyra over working on our marriage.

After another explosive fight where police reported to the scene, I decided to kick Luke out of the house and got a restraining order. As far as I was concerned, this was the end of my marriage. I was tapped out emotionally.

While Luke was going to his mandated anger management classes, the group facilitator reached out to me inviting me to attend a support group for women of domestic abuse. The first night I attended, I was nervous. There were women from all walks of life. After everyone introduced herself, a professional woman began with sharing her testimony. Then each woman went around and shared her personal story as well. There were striking similarities: the small insults and accusations, the isolation imposed by their husband, and the self-doubt that would arise after being blamed for causing the man's unacceptable behavior.

All of them were describing my relationship with Luke to a tee.

After so many years of anxiously walking on eggshells, it was a breath of fresh air to be able to let my hair down knowing that I wouldn't be running into Luke at every turn. Kyra encouraged me to embrace my newfound independence. The first night she and I hit the bars, it was a refreshing change of pace and reminded me of my days as a carefree fourteen-year old spending summers discovering the nightlife in Wyoming with Patty and Dylan. With my self-esteem so battered in my struggles with Luke, it was nice to hear compliments that came my way.

When I decided to embrace my single status again, flirting with the opposite sex was like getting on a bicycle again. While I was a bit rusty at first being in the dating pool again, with Kyra by my side, I was able to enjoy myself. I found myself thoroughly withered under the weight of Luke's paranoia throughout the years of our turbulent marriage.

Luke had found his own apartment by then, and we'd

established a living arrangement for our kids. While we were technically separated, he still had a powerful grip on me psychologically. One time, when he found out that I'd been putting some effort into maintaining a healthy social life, he outright threatened me with, "If I ever find you with another guy, I'll kill you." In his mind, we were far from over.

These deadly words were coupled with words meant to bait me and keep me wriggling on the hook. "No one's ever gonna accept you the way I do. No man is gonna want you with three kids and baggage." His words were meant to plant doubts in my head, and they did.

I was constantly weighing the pros and cons of staying or leaving; the negotiation was never-ending. His controlling nature afflicted our daily lives but I found him accepting of my depression, my periods of dissociation, and my hyperviligance with our kids. I sometimes believed he felt more secure when I depended on him through my bouts of self-loathing.

Because everything in my life was filtered through the lens of my trauma, I truly felt like a crazy person. During moments of great self-doubt, when I found myself against the ropes, I told myself, *No one's gonna love me with all my demons.* I'd get myself so worked up that I would often find myself saying aloud the very words he'd instilled in me.

One evening my best friend Kyra observed his intimidation first-hand. I'd called her earlier in the evening for some advice. When Luke told me, out of the blue, that he wanted to meet me alone at his apartment, my instincts told me that our conversation might take a turn for the worse. However, he still had power over me, and I felt the obligation to go.

Kyra, who could tell I was upset and knew I'd had a few beers, thought otherwise. Wisely, she offered, "Why don't you come over *here* and get ready?" This was Kyra's way of buying me some time to convince me not to meet up with Luke, which could be a potentially deadly situation.

Once we were face to face she told me, "If you go over there tonight, with both of you drinking, it might get out of hand."

Kyra was taken aback when she saw me putting on my make-up and shaving my legs as I told her, flippantly, "If he does kill me, at least I'll look good. This will be the last time."

There was an expression of true fear on her face when I met her eyes. My best friend's reaction was sobering. Then, she said, as steadily as possible, "This isn't going to end well."

I responded, not quite knowing the meaning of my words, "I'm already prepared for that." She later told me that the finality of my words made her blood run cold. Eventually, Kyra was able to convince me to stay in for the night.

Luke, however, was disappointed enough to leave his apartment and track me down at Kyra's house when I didn't arrive as expected. It wasn't hard to guess where I might have been because Kyra was just two houses down from me.

When he showed up, he asked me to step outside and talk to him. I refused, and told him as calmly as possible, "I don't want to talk tonight. We'll meet another time when we're not drinking." I could tell he was inebriated.

Not one to be easily rejected, he didn't like hearing me say no to him. He got mean, and Kyra stepped in to defend me.

Kyra kept telling him, "You're not welcome here. Shelly doesn't want to talk to you. Get lost!"

He screamed back, "I want to talk to my wife, you dirty cunt!" Pretty soon, he was pounding on her door and windows. Finally, he relented after Kyra told him she was calling the cops. He didn't need another incident on record.

Kyra kept her distance after that. Seeing up close and personal how Luke's aggression could escalate to dangerous levels, she truly feared for my life because her repeated concerns for my personal safety fell on deaf ears. While Kyra most likely saved my life that night, it would be another six years before I left Luke for good.

36

WE STAY IN OUR OWN TREE

After a long separation, Luke promised that if I gave up my friendship with Kyra that he would go to marriage counseling. I had to make a choice. I ultimately chose my marriage and I would not see Kyra again until years later. When we did finally reunite, we both wept when we saw each other, and we were able to pick up right where we left off. It was as if we had never stopped being friends.

Sick of the marital strife, I hoped marriage counseling would be a magic wand. But Luke was a reluctant spouse, and I could never get him to go consistently. I wanted a therapist to show him that his paranoia was all in his head. I'd given him no concrete reason to distrust me, which is why I hoped and prayed that the counseling would be effective.

Before long, we'd stopped going to counseling and the abusive cycle would start up again: tension would build, the verbal attacks would start up, a violent outburst would occur, followed by a period of remorse which often included a shifting of blame, and the promise that it would never happen again.

When I got myself back into counseling, I found myself scared and anxious in those initial sessions. I'd gone with the intention of working on my marriage, but when the counselor specifically began asking me about my childhood, I still couldn't recollect much. It's only with ongoing counseling that the fog of my childhood began to lift and then slowly become more transparent to me.

When I began to remember flashes here and there, during my waking hours, the images scared me so much that I went into a mode of full denial. When I was triggered, I made elaborate explanations telling myself that what I was recalling couldn't possibly be real. There's a flash of Damien fondling my breast. In another flash, Damien's on top of me in the sand dune where I would play as a child. The monster's face, with its formerly indistinct features, is now plainly recognizable to me as my brother's.

Going to counseling also precipitated night terrors. In some of my terrors, I'm in a locked room with Damien and I'm screaming to be let out. Far from being my captor, Damien is sitting idly by staring at me. It's as if we're both prisoners locked inside.

In another night terror, Damien and I are being swept away in the rapidly moving current of a river. I'm trying to swim laterally towards the river bank, but Damien is clinging to me for dear life and he's unwittingly drowning me in the process. I woke up screaming from that one after drowning in a tide of blackness. It didn't take me long before I decided to quit going to therapy.

I doubled down on trying to pretend in order to keep my new perceptions at bay. It was incredibly exhausting living in a state of make-believe. The emotional toil on my day to day life was wearing me down. Then, the flashes started coming one after the other like a stacked deck of cards. I was suffocating under the weight of the new revelations. My kids, whom I've always lived for, helped me through the madness. I still had to get up in the morning and show up for my kids. They were my saving grace.

Abstaining from alcohol while I was pregnant with Noah and Nichole provided mental clarity which gave me the keys to unlocking my past. With parts of my subconscious now unveiled, repressed memories started to come together like individual puzzle pieces forming a greater picture. I was now able to reclaim the pieces of my life which had gone missing for so long. My brain was ready to contend with the abuse.

One completely ordinary day when Luke and I were getting the children ready for bed, I was putting lotion on one of the kids, an entirely routine gesture, when the sensory details of smelling the lotion and seeing the yellow coloring of the lotion triggered a memory. It was of Damien using the lotion on me as lubrication. The vividness of what I recalled made me physically ill, and I threw up.

On another day, hearing an Eagles song on the radio triggered another lost and found memory of me laying on Damien's bed. These were the first significant memories that deciphered for me the monster's identity. I was horrified to know that my abuser was the brother I knew and loved. The image I'd formerly upheld of my brother broke into a million little pieces. The shame and sense of betrayal by a close family member was almost unbearable. My mind rebelled. More denial would soon follow.

When I was ready to finally accept and fully possess all the pieces of my dysfunctional history, it was a huge relief to know that I hadn't hurt anybody, as I'd previously suspected. The parts of my childhood that were huge voids prior to my new awareness began to be accessible to me again, but there were new questions about what I should do with the truth. Should I break the news to my family? Should I keep the truth to myself in order to spare family members additional grief? Would the truth threaten my family ties to such a degree that our strong bonds would be broken? And once the truth was out, how would they handle it?

After months of struggling, I decided that I couldn't take any chances with my nieces' and nephews' safety. Damien was around Patty and Dylan's children all the time; I wanted them to know what Damien was capable of doing. The image of Damien harming one of the kids kept haunting me. I wasn't really worried about Damien's own kids. The thought that he would molest one of his own kids was too horrendous to me to fathom. He was still living on the farm with Emily and their kids; his youngest child was born in the time since he'd moved back. He was now a father of four children.

My deep love of family left me greatly conflicted. While knowing the ravaging effects of incest first-hand, self-doubts began to creep in and took hold of me as I tried to minimize the extent of my own abuse. If I brought to light what I remembered, I was afraid it would rip us apart. My father had always taught me to protect family first, and Damien was family. Tugging me in the other direction, though, were fears that Damien would move on to abuse countless other innocent children.

I called Wendy Lou first, and disclosed everything to her. I was relieved Wendy Lou believed me. She even suggested that it made sense, given all my memory loss. Her support gave me the courage to believe that my truth, if I were to tell others, wouldn't fall on deaf ears.

When I told Patty and Caitlyn, their first reaction was one of shock. Then they started questioning me about what happened and when. I tried to be frank with them and told them, "It's like a puzzle; I am still putting all the pieces together." This answer cast a shadow of doubt over my truthful confession. They said that Damien had problems, but he would never do anything like that. They couldn't imagine that he could do what I was accusing him of. I told them that I needed time to come to terms with what had happened, and I stayed away from the farm for a year. It never dawned on me that they wouldn't believe me.

Patty went home and told Dylan what I'd said. Dylan's words came crashing down like an iron fist. He warned, "Tell her to keep her mouth shut." Patty also told me he wasn't about to lose another brother. Dylan made sure that our dad, who was on one of his many excursions, was never told. What Dylan said hurt me to the core. Patty and Caitlyn dealt with the discord by carrying on as if nothing happened. I questioned whether I mattered to my family. Being disempowered like that left me feeling totally isolated.

The word *incest* carries a stigma all its own. No family wants that brand on their family name, and The O'Briens' were no exception. We lived in a very small community, and people would judge. Keeping up appearances was very important to Dylan; I came to hate him because I caved in the face of his harsh words. Everything that was brought to light, clear as day, needed to be concealed once more. He took away a voice I was just starting to cultivate. I should have put my foot down and demanded to be heard. I should have screamed at the injustice of needing to cover up my pain again. I should have returned to the farm and might have realized earlier that Abby, Damien's daughter, was already at risk.

37

THE DEVIL I KNEW

LOVE / HATE

L uke initially stood by me as I tried to sort out all my memories of the ongoing sexual abuse throughout my childhood years. But somehow I also felt shunned by Luke, as if his knowing that I was a survivor of sexual molestation meant that I was no longer an adequate wife or mother. My belief that I was damaged goods was so deeply ingrained.

I began having chronic stomachaches, and a doctor confirmed that my stomach pain was due to stress-related ulcers. Despite the ongoing stress, I was continuing to do well with my daycare business. While it was a good source of income for us and a healthy social environment for my kids, when Noah was in first grade and Nichole was in kindergarten, I decided to close the daycare and began to look for job prospects outside the home.

I found a good job as a property manager making good money. I started to do well for myself and pretty soon had my own company car and office. When I also expressed an interest in higher education and enrolled in college, Luke told me he was proud of me, at first. But it wasn't long before Luke's fear of abandonment reared its ugly head again. While in college he would complain that I was putting too much time into studying and was neglecting the kids.

The same patterns of abuse were ongoing year after year. Our physical altercations were still a regular occurrence, but I continued to fight back in an effort to defend myself. There were times in which I thought I would kill Luke instead of the other way around. The scrapes and bruises would heal, but the emotional battery, which was often far worse, would leave permanent scars.

Truly a love-hate relationship, I couldn't ever call it quits because he was my emotional anchor. I never doubted that Luke loved me, and he often expressed a desire to get a handle on his anger issues, but he could never win that battle with himself. He was the devil I knew.

While Joey was very emotionally resilient, constant exposure to Luke's anger changed Joey into a more stoic and quieter child. By the time Joey was twelve, he began to struggle with his own anger. One silver lining was that Joey was always finding ways to help me and his siblings. I always told Joey never to interfere when Luke and I were fighting. Asking him to stay on the sidelines, though, created a deep well of anger and frustration within him.

By the time Joey turned fourteen, he took it upon himself to begin defending me. He was beginning to stand his ground as he lost his fear of Luke as an authority figure. Luke was never one to back down easily in the heat of a confrontation. I knew I had to get out of my marriage before something irrevocably bad happened. Years later as an adult, Joey confirmed for me that there were also physical confrontations I didn't know about between the two of them, as I'd always suspected.

My other two children Noah and Nichole were not

spared either. By this time in my twelve-year marriage to Luke, my kids had heard and seen it all. The worst fights. All of it. Always motivated to act in the best interest of my children, I made plans to leave Luke. Noah and Nichole were both still young, at ages six and five. Noah was starting to have behavioral problems with rage at school. Nichole, who was always much more reserved, became very clingy, not wanting to be separated from me for any period of time. Joey, as my oldest, was always very protective of his younger siblings.

School counselors suspected that the turbulence in my marriage which was creating a toxic home environment was really affecting my kids, to their detriment. I felt like I was falling down a dark rabbit hole that I didn't know how to escape from. Separating from my husband was not easy, despite how troubled the marriage was. Breaking apart my family went against every family value that was instilled in me from such a young age.

I realized by the end of our marriage that Luke and I were emotionally codependent to an unhealthy degree. I felt what a heroin addict might feel after hitting rock bottom. I was completely strung out and no longer capable of feeling anything. I knew that any hopes of connubial bliss and a family life together were forever shattered. There had been too many broken promises. He couldn't get a reaction out of me anymore, and I had no more fight left in me.

When I left Luke and my home for what would become a permanent separation and eventual divorce, I left everything at the house except for the kids and our clothes. Because Luke and I had gone back and forth with each other so many times before, and because I'd always held a torch for the happy family life I'd envisioned for us together, I wondered if this last separation had the weight of finality. I continued to feel torn because of my own feelings of loneliness and fear for the future. It was hard to let go of my past to run towards an unknown future.

Luke wanted the kids every other weekend. While Joey's relationship with Luke had deteriorated completely, and Joey didn't want anything to do with him, Noah and Nichole missed their dad terribly. I was crestfallen to know that Joey was once again without a father. As a single mom, I tried to be there for my son emotionally but I was such a wreck myself after the collapse of my second marriage that it was all I could do to just get out of bed and make it to work each day.

It's only after custody visits became routine, that I realized what a huge hole was created when my kids weren't with me. I couldn't handle not being with them, so on those weekends when they were gone, I continued to drink to the point of routinely getting drunk and crying myself to sleep. My life was in shambles and I became a shadow of the person I once was.

Instead of being a carefree teenager like other boys his age, Joey took on responsibilities for Noah and Nichole that were more akin to parenting. I remember one Christmas in which I had zero motivation to get out of bed to go Christmas shopping for Noah and Nichole. Joey somehow got me to the store and picked out all of his siblings' presents. At home, he wrapped all the gifts himself in preparation for the holidays.

I still have a lot of guilt for not getting out of my marriage to Luke sooner. The domestic abuse Joey witnessed was something I should have shielded him from but couldn't. Having my son see me at my most vulnerable had a profound effect on him.

Joey had to grow up fast, and I've often wondered, but at what cost to him? I've always wished that I was a better mother to him. Regrettably, he saw a beer in my hand all too often during the throes of my binge drinking, but he never had anything but deep reserves of love and understanding for me.

When Joey noticed the vacuum that was left after Luke and I separated, he even had suggestions on how I might go about meeting new people. If it hadn't been for my tech-savvy son, I never would have met Jack, the love of my life.

38

WHO KNEW ?

That year of not seeing my family went by too slowly. My kids missed their aunties, as my sisters' had always showered my kids with their love. Luke and I finally paid a visit to the farm with my kids in tow. Spotting us, Damien walked over from his trailer, in which he was still living with his own family. Dylan had left Damien completely in the dark regarding my accusations. With Dylan's insistence of keeping the family together, I'd discovered that no one had actually confronted Damien about what he'd done to me.

Everyone was acting as if my recent realizations were no big deal, even Caitlyn and Patty. Getting the family back together again was their priority. I, on the other hand, freaked out being in Damien's company and grabbed my kids and ran into Mom and Dad's old bedroom. I was sitting on the bed, very shaken, holding my kids close to me. Damien came to the door, knocked, and opened the door before I could answer. He had a smug smirk on his face, and acted as if everything was okay and nothing was amiss.

He said, "Can I see your daughter?" Nichole was sitting

on the bed, as Damien walked towards her. My maternal instincts immediately went into overdrive, and I felt this rage in me that I hadn't felt in a long time. I looked him in the eye and threatened him with, "If you *ever* look at my kids or touch them, I will destroy you." There was a fleeting look of hurt in his eyes, maybe even hurt surprise. There was a moment of high tension that hung in the air between us, which made both of us realize what was really being said.

He then got defensive and angry and said, "You're such a bitch." As he walked out, and turned his back on me, he added, "Everyone thinks you're crazy." His words momentarily hit their mark, as a tiny ripple of fear and self-doubt ran through me. But with my newfound truth acting as a protective armor, I was finally beyond his reach. He was no longer a terrifying monster; he was a broken, flawed man.

After I started recalling all of my harrowing abuse, I went through a stage where I became enraged with my mother for not protecting me. How could she *not* have known what I was enduring? Much of the time Damien and I, and my mom, were in the same house as the abuse was taking place. I stewed with my anger for months, not being able to confront my mother now that she was gone.

Rather than any reconciliation taking place in my family tree, things began to splinter further and soon we were faced with a major crisis that shook the very foundation of our family. It's during this period that I found the courage to tell my father that I was abused by Damien. I asked Dad if he thought Mom knew what was going on. I never used the word incest because, for a man of his generation, the subject matter was too taboo.

I asked as directly as possible, "Do you think Mom knew about what Damien had done to me?" He took a moment to collect himself, before saying, "No, Daughter; if she had known, she would have put a stop to it." Hearing my dad's words were healing to me, and I found the resolve to let go of my anger. Caitlyn, however, has different thoughts on the matter. When the topic comes up, as it inevitably does, she says, "Mom knew; she was just in denial. Mom always buried her head in the sand."

39

DO YOU BELIEVE ME NOW ?!

W hen Abby told Emily that she didn't like what Damien was doing to her, Emily believed Abby without question. Emily had noticed how Damien always seemed to pull his daughter away from her other activities and friends, in order to spend extended periods of time alone with her. Emily hatched a plan to remove Abby from her dangerous home environment, and after Abby was safely in trusted hands, Emily went to the authorities.

After Damien's arrest, the whole family pulled together and rallied around Abby. Seeing the outpouring of love and compassion for her helped me to forgive my family for their apathy. But part of me wanted to scream, *"DO YOU BELIEVE ME NOW ?!"* I went to the farm to help as much as I could during this crisis.

Initially, Damien wouldn't accept a plea deal. He likely thought the case would come down to Abby's word against his, and, if it did, he was prepared to take it all the way to trial. I just couldn't fathom putting Abby through that. The prosecuting attorney cautioned us that once Abby took the stand she would have to testify and reveal every graphic detail of the abuse she'd endured.

In the week that followed the arrest, I visited Abby at Caitlyn's house and gingerly asked her if she wanted to talk. I shared with her how he'd groomed me from a young age and how he used my love for him as leverage to get what he wanted. I then told her he went from touching to intercourse and how he did it.

Abby said, "Dad did the same things to me." She told me all the things that had happened between them. Her abuse was like listening to a younger version of myself. She, like me, was forced to grow up too quickly. Listening to her, I realized she no longer considered herself a child. She told me, "I never want to see him again!" I felt all this guilt for not protecting her. If I would have raised my voice a little louder and stood up to Dylan, maybe I could have gotten her out sooner. I told her I would do everything in my power to make sure she never had to see him again. She never had to.

In the days following my talk with Abby, I went down to the jail and told the police what Damien did to me. The prosecuting attorney's questions were unrelenting; his probing questions required extremely explicit details. Before then, I'd never used the word incest to describe what I'd been through. It was too unspeakable. While the statute of limitations of the crimes he committed against me had lapsed, the lawyer explained how we were building a credible case against Damien. My testimony would lend credibility to Abby's statements before the court, and would provide the ammunition the legal team needed to put Damien away for a long time.

The attorney advised that it would be more expedient if Damien accepted a plea deal, in which case he would get a maximum of fifteen years in the penitentiary. However if this ordeal did go to trial, with my testimony supporting

Abby, there was the real possibility of Damien receiving a much longer sentencing of up to twenty-five years behind bars. I wanted to act in Abby's best interest. So I decided to do the hardest thing I'd ever had to do up to that point; I would have to face-off with my abuser once and for all.

In a cramped room with a small table and two chairs, the deputy brought Damien into the room. Damien was handcuffed and in an orange jump suit, and wore a defeated look on his face.

He began, brusquely, "What do you want?"

I was half expecting to hear the words: *I'm sorry for what I did. I'm going to get help.* I searched his face for any expression of remorse, but I found none. Feeling a surge of new anger rising in me, I pushed it all down and firmly said, "I'm not here about you and me. I'm here for your daughter."

"Please take the plea. Don't put Abby through a trial after what you've already put her through. You have the power to end this nightmare. Do the right thing. Take the plea."

He squinted at me with narrowed eyes and said, "What's in it for me? I could win at trial."

He was confident, almost cocky. When I heard those words escape his lips, I realized he was not sorry, but rather sorry that he got caught. He was beyond hope.

I was very measured about what I said next. I wanted him to feel the full weight of my words when I said, "I will take the stand. And it won't end well for you when the truth comes out."

I sensed his hesitance. The stakes were high. Collecting himself, he said, "You would never do that to me." He'd banked on my silence all these years and still believed I would never go public with my most shameful secret.

"I'm not a little girl anymore, Damien. I'm stronger now, and I will do anything I have to do to protect Abby."

He had a moment of uncertainty, in place of his former

cockiness. He stood up quickly and without saying another word, walked out. This the last game he and I would ever play. The next day, the prosecuting attorney called and said there would be no trial. Damien took the plea deal and got fifteen years. I never saw Damien again.

40

103° DEGREES

I found my man on Match.com. It was an era when online dating sites were just coming into vogue. Joey encouraged me to get back into the dating pool, and even helped set up my online dating profile. The computer's algorithm matched me with three men: a doctor, an attorney, and Jack, who was the nerdy computer type. Of the three, Jack is the only one I chose to contact.

To my surprise, he wrote back within the hour with a response. From my profile, he knew I was looking for someone to spend time with every other weekend when I didn't have my kids. After two very painful experiences with married life, I just wanted to have some fun. By that point, Luke and I had figured out our custody arrangements for Noah and Nichole. From his profile, I knew Jack was raising two little girls on his own, Ashley and Martha.

When Jack and I first met at the Lake Walk around Lake Superior, I almost ditched him that first day before he spotted me, but hje approached me before I could make a run for it. Feeling so emotionally bankrupt at the beginning of our relationship, the first thing I found myself saying to him was, "Do I look okay?" Jack looked at me with his beautiful blue eyes and said, "You look just fine," with a wink and a grin. I found him easy to talk to.

Over the next few weeks and months, we slowly got to know each other better as I came to trust him as someone who would not abuse me. It helped that he was from a small town, like I was. Soon after, he wanted to introduce me to his girls. I had reservations because I wanted to keep things casual. But eventually when all our kids met each other, it wasn't long after, that all of us took a leap of faith and began life as a family unit. Jack turned out to be the guy I always needed but never knew I wanted. There have been difficult times over the years where we've had to fight for our relationship when life got challenging, but somehow we've always made it work.

In being my partner, he's filled my emotional needs in a way that I hadn't recognized before as actual needs. When Jack first told me, "I love you," it would be months before I could finally say it back. He was fearless in how he expressed his feelings for me time and time again.

When he accepted me, he also accepted what my family's meant to me and he's never isolated me from the strong and loving bonds I have with Patty, Caitlyn, and Wendy Lou. When they met him, they liked him unanimously. Even my nephews who had grown fiercely protective of me in the aftermath of all I'd endured in my abusive second marriage, gave him their seal of approval. He was in.

When my dad commended Jack on his ability to provide for our large family, it was his way of saying that he liked Jack. Dad, who was still clocking miles on his many road trips up until the last year of his life, would, true to form, pull into our driveway for a surprise visit. Dad's RV would announce his presence, and the grandchildren were always delighted by the sight of it. They would run to Dad as soon as he arrived; he was a natural with our kids. Each grandchild would hear Dad say, "I love you, Young Man," and "I love you, Young Lady." He got into the habit of carrying candy in his pockets. Sometimes, during these surprise visits, it would make for a hairy situation for Jack and me, as we'd never know how many days he planned to stay while he recharged his electric RV. Jack was always a good sport, very unselfish, and welcomed these visits from family.

Another key aspect of how Jack's supported me over the years is that, while he's great at reading me, he's learned to give me the time and space I've needed to figure things out on my own. As our trust level grew, he began dropping hints that we should tie the knot. He would ask me a thousand different ways. We'd be doing something mundane like doing the dishes, and he'd drop the corny line, "Do you want to be my ball and chain?" I replied "nope" many, many, times. This never dissuaded him.

As it would turn out, *I* would eventually pop the question when Prince Charming was bedridden with a 103° flu. It was a chaotic December night with our kids. They were doing homework; I was getting dinner on the table. All of a sudden, a bright lightbulb went off in my head and I just *knew* this was the family I wanted for the rest of my life. What Jack and I had together, with all the chaos, and everything it entailed, was everything I wanted.

I ran into our bedroom, and I jostled him and told him to wake up. He was still coming to his senses, but I had to get the words out, "Let's get married on New Year's Eve." I knew I was committed once I heard myself saying the words aloud. He said, "What!?" We were coming up on our one year dating anniversary and I was getting good at reading him too. I could see the thought bubble above his head with the caption, *"After all this time!?"* More awake, he sputters out the words, "You're gonna ask me to marry you when I have a temperature of 103°?" Then he gave me the biggest grin

I've ever seen on the face of a sick man, and he said, "Okay!"

On my wedding day, with all the abundance that had come into my life in the year after meeting Jack and his beautiful girls, I rediscovered a newfound joy in my life that I'd thought I had lost somewhere along the way. My past life in which fear and uncertainty ruled was finally waning.

An hour before Jack and I would say our *I do's* surrounded by our children and family, I'm looking in the mirror and I feel beautiful standing in my shimmering, blue and silver, dress suit. The three most precious women I love in all the world stand by me, and I feel a serene calm within.

Wendy Lou, my bestie and female soul mate, places a delicate, silver comb into my coiffed hair, which she's curled and swept up, with every hair falling perfectly into place. I marvel that I'm sharing this day with someone who knows me better than myself. We've come so far since the days of running carefree in the woods of Donken, and I know Roger is with us in spirit today.

Patty is meticulously painting my toenails; she's chosen a shade of deep shimmering red, and says with a wink, "This better be the last one; we aren't doing this again." Patty taught me so much about how to have fun and how to enjoy life's better moments. She's always had a wicked sense of humor.

Caitlyn hands me my bouquet of blue flowers in one hand, and places a stiff drink in my other hand with the remark, "Three's the charm!" Caitlyn's the one who's always picked me up when I've fallen, and she's never left my side during the most challenging times of my life when I've felt broken. She was my refuge, and was always there to lend me her strength when I felt my weakest. She's always reminded me that family comes first and her love is a testament to that commitment.

Between the four of us, there's nothing we haven't

shared with each other. Popping the cork, we open a bottle of celebratory champagne and share a wedding day toast with all of us simultaneously squealing with joy, "Let's get married!!" With everyone I love by my side, I step boldly into my future.

41

UNWORTHY OF PAROLE

Though Jack is the love of my life, the trauma doesn't go away. Because I'm in a marriage where the emotional security my husband gives me is the bedrock of our trust, I know that as I evolve in relation to my past trauma I'm better equipped to deal with my history. Knowing I have the support of a man who loves me helps me to battle my fears.

After years of feeling beholden to pleasing and charming behaviors around unworthy men which often led to further personal trauma, I was finally with a man who accepted all of me. I was done pretending.

He knows my history, all of it, and isn't scared to love all of me. While reliving trauma can feel like a never-ending movie, I've now learned as a survivor how to press pause or turn the volume down.

When I become lost in my thoughts, Jack often catches me with a simple, "Come back to me, hon." Jack was by my side throughout the ordeal of me reliving the pain of my past again and again every time Damien would come up for parole.

In the time immediately following his sentencing, my

family at the farm erased him from every conversation of our past memories and took every material possession he had and destroyed all of it so there'd be no visible trace of him on the farm.

When Damien was arrested, my dad was out west on one of his many trips. Even though the secret was out, what happened was so taboo that we hardly knew how to talk it, even amongst family members. Dad was informed, but we never dared broach the subject with him. If Dad made the decision to turn a blind eye, so would we, out of respect for The Old Man.

Dad asked for no details on the length of the sentence or any location details of where his son was serving time. It was like Damien had died. We'd intended to move on as a family without him, and we did. Seven years went by quickly, but when parole hearings put my family in fresh distress, everyone looked to me for guidance on what to do next.

It pained Jack to see the detrimental effect this had on me. While I no longer considered myself a victim, as it had been a long time since I was under Damien's thumb, I was reliving the memories of my sexual abuse in technicolor. I'd have anxious dreams which brought back the night terrors. When the nightmares became a regular occurrence, I would drink and then take an Ambien which had the instant effect of putting me to sleep. I'd always hope that I would sleep through the night. When I didn't, Jack would hold me and comfort me through it all.

My brain also started playing tricks on me during my waking hours in which I would see Damien everywhere. Though I rationally knew he was behind bars, I'd see his face in the crowd and believe that it was him. If I thought I saw him on the street, I'd have to take a closer look to confirm he wasn't actually in the area stalking me.

Damien would come up for parole every year and then every six months in the last year of his sentence. When my family began receiving letters from the parole board, it was very distressing for all of us. It read that the inmate would have a hearing to reduce the remainder of his sentence. Not saying Damien's name or talking about what he did had put a band-aid on our psychic wounds for the first seven years Damien served, but we'd never dealt with the gravity of his betrayal and its ultimate effect in fracturing our family.

My family was so distraught that I felt an enormous responsibility to keep Damien behind bars. I encouraged everyone in our family, including Abby, to write letters the first time he came up for parole. The letters detailed our conviction that Damien was beyond rehabilitation and that he would remain a threat to public safety. Abby's letter explicitly stated that she no longer considered herself his daughter. She chose to never see him again and is now a thriving adult who is married with a son.

The letters I wrote tried to make a case for all the reasons Damien was unworthy of parole. Abusing Abby when he was already an adult and a father to her, he'd made a conscious choice to continue abusing. His daughter was only seven years old, the same age as I was when he began grooming me. He went on to take her virginity as well. Whatever ambiguity there was about how much Damien could be accountable for his criminal acts when he was an adolescent, by the age of twenty-six, when he started grooming his own daughter, there was no question. He'd become who he was through and through; he was an adult predator.

My words also made an impassioned case that during his most formative years as an adolescent, Damien never learned the lessons of accountability or consequence. He was accountable to no one, least of all himself. Being abused by Glen, remaining largely undisciplined by a father who was physically absent much of the time, and not having his older brothers nearby who might otherwise have been male role models for him, it was a perfect storm for the makings of a predator. I argued to the parole board that all throughout Damien's youth and adolescence he was self-absorbed to a fatal degree, and as a result, I made the case that Damien is incapable of expressing empathy as an adult. However, the black and white statements in my letters don't tell the whole story. The actual truth has more shades of gray.

My letters were fueled by the immense hurt I witnessed my family members enduring. I was also writing out of a deep personal pain, and my written words were intended to inflict as much pain as possible towards my brother. What I didn't include in those letters was the understanding I now have in that Damien remains a threat to anyone who is in his inner circle, namely, his family members. *His predation is exclusively incestual.*

His poor social skills, which he never got a chance to develop due to the dire isolation of the farm we grew up on, led to a habitual practice of looking to his immediate family members to fill his normal adolescent sexual needs. His social handicaps make him a threat primarily to his family, unlike a sexual offender who gets caught abusing perfect strangers.

The peculiarities of our family dynamics enabled him to normalize the incest in his own mind and he never perceived it as a crime. As an adult, he minimized what happened by saying, "Yah, we all messed around." In fact, he often argued that what we did was an expression of love for each other. He would tell me repeatedly, "This is what people in love do."

Damien knew exactly how my father would handle familial problems. Damien, like I, heard my father always saying, "We stay in our own tree." We all heard this regularly and towed the line. This is how we protected each other in our family. My dad would never air our dirty laundry and Damien knew this which enabled the abuse to continue. My eldest brother also shared my dad's mentality; for Dylan, saving face was a point of pride. Even for a crime as heinous as incest. Dylan was the one who silenced me into a state of quiet submission when I first came out. I kept my mouth shut for a year, and I might never have had the fortitude to truly confront Damien if he hadn't gotten arrested. The whistleblower who ultimately got Damien behind bars, and put an immediate stop to Abby's ongoing suffering, was not an O'Brien. It's a good thing Emily went straight to the authorities after Abby confided in her.

Mom and Quint, the two cherished family members who might have been instrumental in helping Damien reflect on the moral wrongs of abusing his own daughter, were not there to hold him accountable. Without the healthy checks and balances only Mom and Quint would have been able to provide Damien, his deviance went unchecked. Damien needs to report to a parole officer for the rest of his life; hopefully this measure of accountability will keep him from abusing others.

42

ASHES IN THE WIND

The day a fire ravaged the home that my grandfather had built, it was twenty below in Michigan. Jack and the kids and I were in the area picking up our repaired Suburban which had broken down a few weeks back when we were visiting family. Before heading back home, we decided to stop by the farm. As we turned the corner onto the long road leading up to the farm, I was the first to see flames engulfing the house with smoke coming from the roof. I felt like I was in a movie and time slowed down; I couldn't believe what my eyes were seeing. This couldn't be real.

Overtaken by shock, I stopped the car and ran toward the house screaming and then sobbing. My nephew Bobby, who had been sleeping inside the house, awoke from a deep sleep to a room full of black smoke. He'd called 911, but because our farm was so secluded, it would be well over two hours before the fire department arrived. We had to sit there on pins and needles watching it burn. Patty and Dylan would only arrive later.

Before the fire spread to all parts of the house, I went in to see if I could salvage some essential papers for Patty, and hopefully recover their photo albums. When I walked through the front door into the living room, I crossed a room already foggy with smoke, and cautiously made my way to the kitchen trying to get to Patty's filing cabinet which contained her important documents before the fire engulfed the first floor.

Upon seeing that one corner of the kitchen ceiling had already collapsed, and after feeling the penetrating heat, I knew better than to further risk my safety. I stopped at the threshold of the front door and looked back to take in one last time what was so familiar to me before it all turned into a fiery inferno. Through the smoke, I swear I saw Mom and Quint. Sure of what I saw, I screamed their names. They responded with smiles and then waved to me before disappearing. I wondered if their spirits were now set free.

The whole town turned up to watch the blaze. Those in the volunteer fire department, many of whom were people we grew up with, were trying to extinguish the fire late into the night. It was twenty below zero, a brutally chilly January day, and their lines kept freezing. When the water tanks on the fire trucks were emptied, additional fire trucks arrived from neighboring towns. The farmhouse my Grandpa had built was made of solid brick and it took three days for it to burn out.

Was it fate that I happened to be here to witness the fire consume the home which was the setting of my stolen childhood? We shared so much of our lives together in this house, would there be anything left of our legacy to speak of after the house was gone?

Seeing the impressions of Mom and Quint emanate from the smoke, I felt like I had the chance to finally say goodbye to both of them. There was no more fantasizing; I could finally let go and know they were in a better place. The part of me which now recalled all of the forgotten memories surrounding my abuse was glad that the walls which had once kept secret those horrible acts had now gone up in flames. All that remained were ashes, which scattered in the wind.

Not long after the fire, we also lost Aunt Jesse. I got the phone call from Patty one evening that Aunt Jesse, whose health had been declining rapidly, was at death's door. Rushing to her side, I found her unconscious when I arrived. I sat with her all night holding her hand, and singing her favorite song, *The Green Green Grass of Home* by Tom Jones.

She always believed she would see all her many sisters in heaven, including my mother. That evening, while I found her unresponsive, I prayed that she could hear me. I begged for her forgiveness about the horrendous things Damien had done to her and all the things I hadn't done for her at the time of her sexual violation. I was too young to know better. I also apologized to her for not being able to take care of her longer than I did when she was in my custody.

This was my first time being beside a family member just hours before death. While I had grown to accept that Mom and Quint had passed away long ago, this was my closest encounter with death. I held her hands which were so alarmingly cold that I rubbed them compulsively.

The kind nurses who attended to her looked at me with sad eyes and said that is was part of the process. I held her hands all night and listened to her breathing, always afraid that she'd taken her last breath. At 7:08 am the following morning, my Aunt Jesse started to struggle to breathe. I was in a panic and screamed for the nurse. The nurse again had to come in and reassure me that this process of letting go was natural and expected.

Not ready to lose Aunt Jesse, I couldn't cope and started sobbing as Aunt Jesse drew her last breath. I was crying not just for her but for everyone I'd lost before their time. Tears that I never once allowed myself to shed for Mom and Quint came in a torrential outpouring of emotion, like the walls of a dam had broken. I sensed a wave of heat leaving her body, which I interpreted as the separation of her soul from her body. But before her soul's departure for the great beyond, I was given a final gift of peace which enveloped me and comforted me as I gazed at her limp body, now an empty shell. The last of the Breeden sisters was gone. Just like my mom, there was no memorial, and no funeral. She simply was no more. Both of them live on now in the retelling of my story and in my memories.

43

LETTERS OF APOLOGY

Damien served his time, and when he was a free man he chose to move far away from the Upper Peninsula and made a new life for himself downstate. There was not only outrage from the family, but there was a community outcry as well. The whole town knew of Damien's offenses. The vitriol was real, and Damien's very life would be endangered if he had dared to return to the area. He knew better.

While Damien is no longer in touch with his biological children, he's successfully created a new family around him. We believe that those who are currently in his life know nothing about his past, and we assume that Damien wants it to stay this way. Damien was offered a chance to be a participating voice in my life's story. I would have valued the insight, as it could have given me answers to questions only he could give. However, he declined the offer, by saying, "I have a new life now. I want to leave it in the past." It makes me wonder if he's ever acknowledged his culpability in what happened. Never once did he admit to what he did. Never once did he use the word incest. It went unnamed.

Patty was outraged and found Damien abusing his own daughter as an unforgivable act. Patty, who was extremely close to Abby, carried a strong sense of guilt that she didn't notice signs of Abby's distress any earlier than the day of Damien's arrest. While Damien was sentenced to a maximum prison sentence of fifteen years, he only served ten. We assume he received mandatory counseling during his time behind bars, though it's unconfirmed, and we do not know if he reconciled his own experience of sexual abuse by Glen.

While he claimed that he's sorry for any hurt that he's caused, I can attest that I know Damien through and through. And I know him all too well. In a letter that he wrote to us, Damien wants us to believe that he's remorseful. When in fact, I believe he's only sorry because he got caught. Never once in his letter does he mention that he was wrong or voice the criminal nature of his actions. The letter read:

Shelly:
I never apologized before because I didn't think anybody would want to hear it, or believe me.

Deep in my heart, and in every fiber of my being, I'm sorry for everybody I hurt.

If giving up my life would set everything straight and give everybody closure, I would not hesitate. I'm not asking for forgiveness because I don't deserve it.

These were the very same words Damien had used as a teenager whenever he was caught for a misdeed. I've heard a variation on the same theme numerous times in the past throughout my life. This letter, which could be addressed to anyone, does not show evidence of a changed heart, and, there's no indication that he has received or ever planned on getting help.

Dylan was the most forgiving of Damien. Slowly, they rekindled their relationship as brothers in the years since Damien's release. Though it still upsets Patty when Dylan talks to Damien, Dylan defends him by saying, "He will always be my brother; he's family."

When the homestead my grandfather built went up in flames, Patty and Dylan lost everything. They took over the farm in the years after our mother passed away and after my father resumed his life on the road. They made sure he would always have a home to come back to. After the fire, they had to literally rebuild their lives.

Damien sent a letter with some money to Dylan and Patty to help out with the reconstruction after the fire. Patty took such overtures as a ploy to get back into our good graces. Patty, Caitlyn, and I were so livid, and we thought we'd write one final letter spelling out how unwelcome he was. I knew his prison sentence alone wouldn't break him. Filled with righteous anger, I was now at a point where I truly wanted to break his spirit.

Of all the mind games he'd played with me over the course of our lives, I was determined to win this hand. Without thinking of the consequences of my words, I wrote, "When I say you don't have a family anymore, that includes Dad. You broke his heart. He is so ashamed of you and says he doesn't have a son named Damien anymore, and that you're dead to him."

Dad never said those words. A few years after that letter, when my dad was seventy-five years old, the whole family was gathered at the new house we'd rebuilt after the fire. My dad had joined us in conversation, mostly listening to us talking about Damien. Looking over at him, I saw that he was deep in thought and asked him what was on his mind. He responded, "Damien is only human. He made a big mistake, and he's paid for those mistakes." Until that admission, I had assumed my dad had taken my side. For him, it wasn't about taking sides at all.

I then asked him if he missed Damien, and he looked at me with tears in his eyes and said, "He's my son, Daughter, of course I miss him. I love him."

Hearing my dad say that, I was floored. The fresh guilt hit me like a ton of bricks. He obviously wanted to see his son again. I wasn't able to forgive myself for the words that I'd put into my father's mouth. Now I knew the true cost of my words, I regretted the time that my father lost with a son he never stopped loving. In retrospect, I wish I had handled my vengeance more honorably.

When I saw my Dad next, I came clean with what I did and was reduced to tears when I told him. He took my hand and said in a stern but reassuring voice, "Daughter, it's okay, I forgive you." I told Dad I would right the wrong I did. In the days that followed, I wrote Damien and said I had no right to speak for our father. I told him I was sorry for misleading him and gave Damien our dad's phone number.

A couple of weeks after that, Dad and Damien started communicating and would continue to do so for the remainder of Dad's life. You could tell talking to his son brought him closure, which brought with it its own kind of peace. I told my Dad I didn't want to know anything about his recent correspondence with Damien. After some time had passed, though, my Dad, being who he was, would try and bring Damien up "accidently" in conversation. He wanted his family back together.

My dad didn't realize the full scope of my trauma. And one day when he was talking on his phone, he handed it to me and asked me to say hello. Not knowing who he was talking to, I took the phone and said, "Hello?" After hearing

Damien's voice, I dropped the phone and sought refuge in another room, trying to soothe myself by reflexively rocking back and forth. My family tells me I was just *gone* for a period of fifteen minutes in which I was mumbling words like, "not here" and "go away". When I came to, I was surrounded by the concerned faces of my husband Jack, Wendy Lou, Caitlyn, and Patty. They had all been calling my name and told me that I wouldn't respond and that I was hyperventilating. My response of post-traumatic stress in reaction to hearing Damien's voice was instantaneous; it took a couple days after that to recover.

44

THE BARRY BUNCH

With Jack as my spouse, I've come to know what healthy intimacy is all about. When Jack and I fell in love, it was a slow burn; it differed from my failed marriages because our love was not an explosion of fireworks that ignited quickly before fizzling out. Falling in love with my husband, gradually, allowed Jack to earn my trust. Sixteen years into our marriage and going strong, my love for him has grown over the years. It's very possible that I fall in love with him more each year.

Our wedding symbolized a union of two families becoming one. Jack and I had made a commitment not just to each other but to our children. I had no doubts about Jack being a great husband, and I already knew he was a good father to Ashley and Martha when I finally agreed to marry him. By that time, a year into our relationship, Jack's kids and I had developed a deep love for each other. When we all started living together, Ashley and Martha started calling me MommaShell and it soon became Mom.

I will never forget the first time I met Ashley and Martha. They had big blue eyes like Jack. Absolutely adorable and naturally curious, when they asked who I was,

I told them I was a friend of their Dad's. You could tell they craved a mother's touch, and the first time we bonded was when the girls crawled into my lap as I read them books.

Martha, who was only four, was on my hip from Day 1. She bonded with me instantly, and fell in love with her new siblings. She had no problems adjusting, and she felt at home right away. As the littlest one of our kids, she was always trying to get her voice heard.

During the few times her biological mother did come into the picture, Martha made her preferences known. When Martha was still quite young, we were at the Minneapolis airport in which we'd arranged a month-long stay with their biological mother in Florida for both of the girls. When it was time for her mom to take Martha from my arms to board the plane, Martha began screaming and buried her face into my neck, turning away from the sight of her mother. Tensions were running high, and I'd never seen her so distressed. She pleaded with me, "Momma, don't make me go." Her biological mother relented, and we decided it was best to let Martha remain.

When we announced to the kids we were getting married, we sat everyone down together to break the good news. Everyone was happy for us except Ashley who promptly broke into tears and ran out of the room. When I asked her what was wrong, she said, "If you and Dad are getting married, that means that you'll leave us and we'll never see you again." That's what she thought getting married meant, and it broke my heart. I then explained to her that her Dad and I getting married meant that I was never going to leave her. She broke into a big smile. Still, whenever I'd step out to go to the grocery store Ashley would have severe separation anxiety. She would beg and cry for me not to go because she always thought I was abandoning her. It was a few years before those jitters went away.

Joey, who was fifteen when I met Jack, had really come into his own. My son was no longer a young boy. He was a young man who often called himself the man of the house. He was also a protector for his siblings Noah and Nichole and after Jack and I were married, Joey's love overflowed and his nurturing side included Ashley and Martha. With a blended family that included four younger siblings in which Joey was still the oldest, he was always there to lend a helping hand. In many ways, our large family prepared Joey for fatherhood.

My meeting and falling in love with Jack was an adjustment for Joey, who was always there for me during the rockier times of my former marriages. Through everything he'd witnessed and experienced alongside me, Joey had earned the right to be a little cautious around Jack. But eventually Joey and Jack bonded over activities like multi-player videogaming and recreational sports like snowmobiling, four wheeling, and motorcycling. Joey discovered he could come to depend on Jack, as a son would depend on a father.

When Joey came to the realization that Jack was a worthy and capable man who loved me, it was very freeing for Joey. It allowed Joey to shed his adult responsibilities. Jack was a fixture in our lives now, and Joey was able to enjoy a second chance at being a normal happy teenager.

By the time Joey was sixteen, he was used to doing what he wanted. After I met Jack, I got back into full-time parenting mode and when I found out Joey was skipping school, I took a few days off of work and I sat through all his classes with him. I followed him around campus all day. He was mortified and I told him the next time I found him skipping school, I would show up on campus wearing a very short skirt. This worked for a while to reinforce him, but I always needed to stay two steps ahead of him. The mischief he'd been so good at finding as a child was now on full display.

When I noticed that my son was starting to experiment with alcohol himself, I wanted to beg him to exercise moderation and not to party too hard, but what could I say in my defense when I'd been such a poor role model? Sometimes, I think Joey felt utterly rootless growing up. I feared there was no foundation grounding him. When Jack and I married each other, Joey finally had the emotional security to know that he would have two parents championing him through thick and thin.

It was not all roses. After the honeymoon stage, the actual day to day work of integrating our children into one big family was extremely challenging. From day one we made it clear there were no stepsisters or stepbrothers, only brothers and sisters. Nichole, who was used to being the only girl, and whom I'd always called my little princess, was threatened by the idea that she no longer had my sole attention.

When Noah began to get along famously with Martha, Nichole, who'd always considered herself Noah's twin, felt like she was suddenly playing second fiddle. There were some royal tantrums. In some ways, this was the first home environment in which Nichole's true feelings could surface. As time passed, Nichole and Ashley, who were the same age, found the perfect playmate in each other and seemingly shared everything.

Because Luke and I shared joint custody of the kids, every other week both Noah and Nichole would go to their Dad's. While there, they continued to witness Luke's abusive outbursts and often unpredictable behavior. It became so toxic for both Nichole and Noah that when they'd return home after a week away, they often brought confusion back with them.

Seeing my kids so changed on a week to week basis

really rattled me and I sought outside help from counselors who informed me that their anger was normal, given their experiences. Noah's early childhood, in particular, was marked by anger. Seeing such aggression in my son, I enrolled him in a wonderful school called Little Learners, in which they showed Noah different ways to channel his aggression. The tools Noah was given worked for many years. Later, when Noah was older at the age of nine, ongoing confusion about divided loyalties between his dad Luke and me often fueled new bouts of resentment.

What would begin as horseplay and monkeying around would soon escalate into a no holds barred pummeling match in which Noah threw punches when his temper got out of hand. Once he got worked up, we often had to restrain him until he calmed down, which broke my heart. Eventually, Jack and I were successful in learning how to help Noah manage his emotions better.

Once our girls became teenagers, they were hellraisers. Our house was the designated place to hang out and with all of our kids' friends at our place nearly all the time, life in our home was a constant circus. Noah went through his own teenage rebellion, and Joey was beginning to find his footing as our first child who would move out to begin life as a full-fledged adult.

As our kids became young adults, we were still supporting four kids under our roof, and it got to the point where Jack and I really felt the strain on our marriage. After this continued for a few years with no relief, Jack and I were at a breaking point. Jack kept trying to convince me that our kids were adults now and they needed to be on their own. We couldn't keep up with the rising costs. None of them paid for anything and no one helped out around the house. I would come home after work to a pig sty and have to make dinner for the whole brood. It was unsustainable and by the time our kids were eighteen, I put my foot down.

Thankfully, they were all out of the house after two months. Noah and Nichole moved into a place together, and Ashley moved into her first apartment. Jack and I were there every step of the way and helped each of them with their transition into adulthood. Martha, our youngest, stayed at home with us as she prepared for college.

Finally, some peace! Jack and I were initially happy to have the house all to ourselves for the first time in years. Life was grand for the first few days, but then we started feeling the deafening silence of our empty nest. My kids, who were always my everything, and who kept both Jack and me on our toes all these years, were gone.

The wild plans we'd made while envisioning our life post-kids, including wild sex in every room of the house, and being able to take trips at the drop of a hat, never materialized. The unnerving quiet which descended on the house left both Jack and me not knowing what to do with ourselves; our transition from full house to empty nest was very emotional for the both of us.

When I missed my kids, I would wait for them to call me instead of picking up the phone to call them. It was advice I'd learned from my mom long ago that somehow stuck. While Jack would never admit to missing the kids, I could see that he was feeling stuck as well; he dedicated too much time to his gaming addiction. Sometimes I felt like Jack and I were two ships passing by each other in the night.

45

THE EVOLUTION OF SEX

Married to Jack for the last sixteen years, our sex life has evolved alongside our relationship. In the beginning, it was paramount to me that my husband was satisfied in our sex life. Being good at sex and meeting all of Jack's sexual needs was still the main factor in my own sense of emotional security within my marriage. After I knew, beyond the shadow of a doubt, that Jack loved me for who I was, and not what I did, I was able to adopt a much healthier view of sex with my husband. My comfort level with him skyrocketed.

With the love Jack gives me, my self-esteem is no longer tied to my sexuality as it had always been for so many years. My sexuality is no longer weaponized.

A part of my mentality as a survivor is the strong desire to hide the effects of my abuse, especially from my husband. This was true for all three of my marriages. I often heard my ex-husband tell me how lucky he felt in comparison to his friends whose wives often had difficulty achieving orgasms. Many wives didn't care for sex at all. Hearing this kind of news only confirmed what I already believed, and I carried these beliefs into my relationship with Jack.

Finding my own enjoyment during sex hasn't always been easy, but remains an evolving aspect of my recovery. After many years with Jack, I have been able to enjoy sexual intercourse, though there are still times when I am triggered. I try to remind myself when Jack and I are physically intimate to stay in the moment. In order to experience the sexual pleasure that comes with orgasm, I initiate a fantasy, and draw on a strong visual picture which helps me stay attuned to my own arousal.

As a mature couple, while we aren't having copious amounts of sex anymore, when we are intimate nowadays it's more meaningful. Sex is now an expression of the love we share as husband and wife.

When I am triggered, there seems to be no predicting the mental pitfalls ahead of time. Sometimes triggers happen, other times they don't but when they do occur, my reaction can vary from extreme revulsion to mild discomfort. In the case of the former, I feel like screaming, *Get off of me!!!* However, instead of scaring Jack and disrupting our sexual experience, and the shared emotional aspects of the intimacy, I've learned how to cope better.

Recovery is a life-long process and I'm at a point where, even though there are shadows of my past, I am beyond the worst of my personal demons. I'm no longer ruled or defined by my abuse.

46

THE MAN OF MANY FACES

W hen my Dad turned sixty, he started feeling sick. He got jaundiced and so bloated from his liver failing. When Patty took him to the emergency room, the doctors told him, "If you have another drink, you will die." He promised to change his ways, but refused any additional care and went home to recover for what was a period of about six months. True to his word, he never had another alcoholic drink again. I wish I could say he was a changed man when he stopped drinking, but much to my regret he wasn't. He still went to the bars, but drank non-alcoholic beer. In the beginning he was what we'd call a dry drunk because the bad temper he was so famous for persisted, but he mellowed out significantly as time passed. In his later years, he became quite the softie.

Nothing seemed to slow down my dad. He continued to travel all over the continental United States in his RV. He went as far west as Washington state to enjoy the incredible scenery of the Pacific Northwest. He spent a lot of time revisiting friends in Butte, Montana and traveled throughout the great state of California. He went fishing in Alaska. He even crossed the border into Mexico and enjoyed the local customs there.

His travel companions, sometimes two at the same time, were almost always female. It was common knowledge that he outlived many of the women he got involved with. As he aged, he kept his good looks and the charm which was so appealing to those women who were drawn to him. Though he stayed on the road most of the year, there were some lean times during which he would stay with one of his grown children. We would help him out if he was broke and enjoyed having him around. It was a great excuse for the grandkids to be able to spend time with their grandpa, but he never stayed long. He always insisted on living this way. He could never stand still for long; he valued his mobility and his freedom above all else.

We saw his personality slowly change over the years for the better. He opened up his heart and was more emotionally available to us. My dad always told us that he loved us growing up but, like my mother, he wasn't always good at expressing himself. It was customary for him to say, "I love you, Daughter" or "I love you, Son". We always found it funny that he never addressed us by name.

Time also changed my own heart in that I'd long since forgiven him for the old resentments I'd once harbored. I was able to re-experience the love I had for him when I was a little girl. Getting to know my father in a way I'd never been able to previously, we became very close and I gained a new appreciation for him in the last ten years of his life.

The most memorable trip I took with Dad was to his hometown, the place where he'd spent his childhood and his formative years. He retraced the route he took to school everyday and we visited the gravesites where his biological mother and his grandparents were buried. It's on this trip that Dad shared so much about his early life and opened up to me in a way he never had before.

He fought tooth and nail to keep driving until the end. Dylan threatened to take my dad's drivers license away so many times but just didn't have the heart to do it. He knew how much my dad relished his freedom on the road. Dad went through so many vehicles from the minor fender benders he would always get into as he got elderly. It was time for him to stop driving but he refused, arguing, "If I can't drive anywhere, then what's the point? I might as well pack it in." Dad was used to getting his way, and this was no exception. He kept driving up until the week he passed away.

The week we lost him, he'd just turned eighty-nine years old, and amazingly, his mind was still sharp. He was staying at the farm with Patty and Dylan. Patty, who noticed he was acting erratically, insisted on taking him to the hospital, where doctors confirmed he'd sustained a couple of small heart attacks. The doctors warned he probably wouldn't survive surgery and that he could have "the big one" at any time.

Receiving this news, my dad refused to stay in the hospital. I begged and pleaded with him, but he was adamant he wanted to spend his last days at the farm, so we took him home. I watched him as he slept and I monitored his breathing each night. Patty, Dylan, Caitlyn, and I were consistently by his side and we spent our final days together as everyone made plans to flock to the farm to be by his side.

"I'm so overwhelmed to know how much everyone loves me," he kept saying over and over again, "I don't deserve this. I don't deserve to be this happy." You could see the tears of appreciation in his eyes. Looking through our family's photo albums, of which there were many, he could still pick out most everyone by name and knew the date and years when the photos were originally taken. The most recent photos were from his eighty-ninth birthday party in September. While he was definitely the oldest soul in the room, the youngest in attendance at the party were his great-grandchildren.

As we held hands in the three days I spent with him in the final week of his life, I felt the adoration and love I once had for him in abundance as a child. He was still trying to convince me that he was still in fighting shape to take one last road trip. To his current girlfriend's no less. Sweet Joyce. Though he no longer had the strength to make the trip, he needed to say the words in order to recapture the love of freedom that defined so much of his life.

My dad was surrounded by his children and grandchildren in his last days. In one of our final conversations, he said to me, with sad puppy dog eyes, "Daughter, I've done some bad things in my life and it's too late to fix them." I looked at his still handsome face and let him off the hook gently, by saying, "It's what you did after those bad things that count, Dad. You learned to love again." His confession took me by surprise. My whole life, he was a formidable figure who was always charging ahead like a bull in a china shop. His mantra had always been, "You can't go back. You always have to move forward." Both of us had nothing but love and respect for each other at this point; we were way beyond rehashing what couldn't be fixed.

In the years after he gave up drinking, he'd lost his mean streak and often got emotional. He was known to give lots of hugs and he made sure he told all of his children and grandchildren, "I love you." To the grandkids who were with him in the last week of his life, he said, as he often did, "I love you, Young Man," and, "I love you, Young Lady."

After my mother's death, Dad had a habit of seeking out conversations with Mom, while in quiet meditation. My dad never stopped loving my mom. Not only was she his soul mate, in the years after her death, he said that she was his spirit guide. He claimed my mom was always talking to him and guiding him. They both believed in past lives, or rather, the need to live your life again if your work here on earth was not finished. In meditation, my mom told him that both of them were now spiritually perfected. They would soon be together forever; I always believed him.

As he got closer and closer to death, I found him talking audibly to Mom again. He asked her what time he would make his final transition and she answered him, "Don't worry about it. Soon." After that he tried to reach her again while meditating, but was getting no further communication from his guide.

The evening he passed away, he said goodbye to all of us. Helping him to his feet, I assisted him with the walker. As he made his way to his bedroom, he suddenly stopped and broke out into a huge grin. He clasped his hands together in relief to see the return of his guide. My heart sank, and I knew my mother was now by his side and ready to claim him. I put a smile on my face for him and said, "Mom's back, isn't she?" He said, "Yes, she is. I'm so happy!"

Moments later, as Patty was getting him to bed, Dad collapsed and had his final heart attack. Caitlyn, Patty, Dylan, and I were not ready to lose him. I was crying, "Daddy, please don't go." Dylan begged, "Please fight, don't give up just yet Dad." Caitlyn stood in shock. My niece and nephew were pleading with Grandpa to hang on. Dad took one last breath; Mom had come to take him home. After he made his final transition, we spread his ashes on the farm in the same field as Mom's. They were now together.

Dad was a man of many faces, who valued freedom and family. He taught us how to love fiercely through the many changing seasons of our family tree. When leaves were barren, our strong roots would anchor us and bind us to each other, for better or for worse. After winter's dormancy, we knew leaves would sprout again and new buds would bloom. While Dad is no longer with us, his legacy lives on.

REBIRTH

I knew when Joey fell in love that it would be for life. That's the way he's always loved. Joey met Amber when he was eighteen and she was sixteen. I liked her instantly, and my comment to her about having baby-bearing hips is now famous in our family. From the very beginning, they were completely at ease and open with each other and complemented each other well. Amber had a calming effect on him, which seemed to help him to better manage his own emotions. We readily accepted Amber as family and, over the years, the strength of their love has prevailed.

Professionally, Joey excelled at electronics and computers. Thankfully, he went into a field where being self-taught helped him to advance. He found his niche, and it didn't require an academic degree.

Amber stood by him as Joey headed into his twenties, when he experimented and then fell into a dangerous habit of using prescription pills. His drug use throughout his twenties robbed him of his great sense of humor, and the most loving parts of himself.

Joey was prone to suppressing his emotions. He'd always

told me it never bothered him that Logan and Luke weren't in his life, but I knew better. I believe his drug use was the primary way he dealt with conflicting feelings.

In our many efforts as a family to get him clean, he went through periods of withdrawal in which I would stay up all night with him. Our relationship was close enough that he would call me when he needed me most.

When Joey finally sought treatment, after he'd hit rock bottom, I was by his side. I learned in counseling with him that my relationship with my kids was so central to my identity that I didn't know how to be without them. Especially Joey. I have to remind myself, more often than not, to let him go and be the man who he aspires to be for himself and his family. Joey's recovery was a long road back to his former self, and Amber was by his side throughout.

It was November of 2016 when I got some news that would forever change my life for the better. My dearest Joey and his wife Amber came over and told Jack and me we were going to be grandparents. I sobbed when they told me, immediately breaking into tears of joy. It would be the next generation of our family. Jack, who has always been more stoic, was grinning from ear to ear.

Seeing my son become a father himself was one of my life's sweetest moments. The day my beautiful grandson Christopher was born, Joey invited us into the maternity room where Amber was bonding with Christopher. All of us had gathered, and we were very excited to meet the newborn addition to our family.

When Joey placed Christopher into my arms, within hours of his birth, my grandson looked up at me, his big eyes already wide open. My world was whole, and I felt the same serene peace I felt when I held Joey for the first time.

With my grandson staring up at me, I felt seen and connected to him in a way I can't explain to this day. It was as if he already knew me, and knew everything about me.

There are no words to describe the spiritual height of that moment. The love I felt for Christopher was enormous.

I was finally able to tell my adult son, "Joey, now you know the love I've always had for *you*." Amber and Joey had tried for a year to have this baby, so Christopher is very wanted. Today, Joey is to Christopher the father he never had, and I know Joey takes great pride in being a father to his child. Like me, he's very overprotective.

Becoming Christopher's grandmother reignited my sense of purpose. Delighting in the love of my grandchild, it's my great joy to see his many firsts. There's no greater fulfillment for me. Seeing Christopher engage the world around him though his senses, it enables me to see the world anew myself.

On our many walks, I learn so much by observing his response to the many wonders of nature. The wind rustling in the trees overhead and the multilayered sound of the many bird calls are accompanied by his squeals of delight.

Watching him jump into puddles, kissing his boo-boos away, telling him I'm going to eat him up like a cookie, and receiving his many hugs as he says, "I love you Nammaw," makes every day I share with him infinitely amazing.

Because I don't have the monumental job of raising him, I spoil him and love him to pieces instead. While I can't go back in time and undo the mistakes I've made with my kids, I can fully embrace the blessings that come with my grandchildren who represent the exquisite budding of new life on our family tree.

I've come to appreciate every season of my life knowing that every loss through the winter season is merely the predecessor to what is reborn in the full bloom of spring.

THE END

AFTERWORD

When I read the following excerpt from a fellow survivor, it resonated with me so powerfully that I felt compelled to highlight the excerpt again here in my book. It is a powerful testament to the lifelong emotional fallout from the abuse of incest:

"Please allow me to say: I am an incest survivor and I have PTSD. This is why my body remembers and I am anxious. This explains all the medications I'm taking. This explains the inexplicable acute manifestation of my inflammatory disease. This can explain that I'm not stupid or forgetful but, in fact, learned to disassociate as a child to protect myself in unsafe environments. Or so that I can explain that I am not crazy or unstable but am falsely wired to worry a lot and frequently and it takes the world to calm myself. Allow survivors to say that so they can continue to fiercely resist and/or recover from addiction to sex, love, cigarettes, food, alcohol, prescription medications, picking skin, soda — you name it. And say it so we can continue to work as hard as I have been working to heal, but not in deep secret, as I had to as a kid to keep someone's secret that hurt me."

-ANONYMOUS[11]

The taboo of incest often underprepares mental health professionals who have inadequate knowledge to recognize the incestual abuse that is often hidden in plain sight. In addition to equipping our professionals, we also need to be directly educating our children by talking to them about their bodies, particularly the hard stuff: there are clear boundaries which should be never be trespassed. Namely, the touching of private parts. It's also important children understand these rules apply to them.

The statistics are startling. With an estimated 80% of all incest occurring between siblings, it occurs much more frequently than incestual abuse between a parent and child. Often dismissed by family members as child's play or experimentation, sibling incest goes underreported and is the least investigated.

The repeated incidents of sexual violation within a sibling incestual relationship can often do much more harm than a one-time sexual assault, because of the sibling's close proximity and access to his or her victim. Entrapment by the instigating sibling often gradually diminishes the victim's ability to refuse further sexual advances.

I encourage parents to risk being overly involved rather than under involved or absent in your parenting. It's critical to know who your children are spending time with and where they're spending the majority of their time. Though you risk embarrassing your children, and they may not forgive you until later, a nosy parent can often make for a good parent when it comes to the safety of our children.

I've often spent time trying to figure out for myself whether Damien was a victim or a predator. What I've come to realize is that he was both. Childhood sexual trauma can manifest in a variety of ways as life unfolds. While my father Liam and my ex-husband Luke did not grow up to be sexual abusers themselves, the long-term emotional effects of their abuse were most evident in their brutal need for domination and control.

Long after the sexual acts between Damien and I ended, I was emotionally crippled. I had no clear picture of what a healthy relationship looked like, and I found myself stuck in a domestically abusive marriage. Being a victim of incestual abuse led to poor disregard of my self-worth which kept me on a spiraling path of self-destruction.

I harbor no ill-will towards my family members for how they chose to handle my disclosure. I deeply understand the culture we grew up in and my family's need to preserve itself. I have long forgiven them for not initially believing me.

Abby's abuse impacted us all, challenging us to become stronger than we've ever been before. She was a shining example of grace under fire, and her courage helped us to truly open our eyes to the vulnerabilities within our family tree. My family has aided in my own recovery in meaningful ways since.

Recovery doesn't happen overnight; it is a journey of a thousand miles. I voice my story for other survivors, and their families, so we will never be silenced by what's too taboo to talk about ever again.

NOTES

1. "Child Sexual Abuse Accommodation Syndrome." *About EDCI*, www.edcinstitute.org/library/120-effects-and-impact/151-child-sexual-abuse-accommodation-syndrome.html.

Summit, R. C. The Child Sexual Abuse Accommodation Syndrome, Child Abuse and Neglect 1983; (7): 177-192

Child Sexual Abuse Accommodation Syndrome: Dr. Roland Summit's theory on how sexually abused children view their abuse and attempt to cope with it.

Secrecy: I learned to keep what was happening a secret. I believed that everything would be okay as long as I kept quiet.

Helplessness: I was brainwashed into believing the sex I was having was consensual. This is often called coercive incest. I was afraid of losing Damien's love as well as the love of my family members.

Entrapment and Accommodation: As a child, I

couldn't understand that someone who claimed to love me, and whom I loved, could also be hurting me. I began fantasizing in childhood, a coping skill that stayed with me through adulthood, and learned how to dissociate from the trauma.

Delayed, Conflicted and Unconvincing Disclosure: Like many children who are abused, I didn't tell anybody until well into adulthood because of my betrayal blindness, which resulted in memory loss.

Retraction: After my family was told, it wasn't talked about and I was largely isolated for nearly a full year. I felt pressure to retract my truth.

2. Kluft, Richard P. "Ramifications of Incest." *Psychiatric Times*, 12 Jan. 2011, www.psychiatrictimes.com/sexual-offenses/ramifications-incest.

The 5 Stages of Abusive Incest:

Stage 1 is engagement. Damien gave me special attention that fed the emotional needs I wasn't getting from my mother. My father was largely absent. Damien gradually normalized the sexual behavior, first introducing sexualized behavior to me as games.

Stage 2 is the sexual interaction phase. Damien's sexual involvement with me escalated from touching to penetration. In order to please him, I went along to get along. I wanted him to be happy.

Stage 3 is secrecy. Damien made me feel responsible for what took place because I initially participated in his games; my secret went untold as the abuse continued to take place and escalated into more explicit acts, which resulted in my deep self-loathing. As his victim, his fatal flaw was his selfish need to satisfy himself, at the cost of my innocence. He made me feel that I was just as guilty as he was. And, if we were found out, I would suffer the consequences. I loved him and didn't want him to get into trouble.

Stage 4 is disclosure. My disclosure did not happen until well past the age of adulthood. My secret was so deeply buried, I remembered nothing of my childhood trauma. While I no longer lived on the farm, our family remained very close-knit. Once my repressed memories surfaced, my sense of familial loyalty and my deep personal shame made disclosure to my family all the more challenging. I only revealed my secret in the interest of protecting my nieces and nephews, who Damien remained in close proximity to.

Stage 5 is suppression of the truth by my immediate family members. My family members believed I was greatly exaggerating. Rather than dealing with the fallout of the damning truth, they acted with a collective interest to preserve our family tree.

3. *(PDF) Trauma at Home: How Betrayal Trauma and Attachment ...* www.researchgate.net/publication/260286688_Trauma_at_home_How_Betrayal_Trauma_and_Attachment_theories_understand_the_human_response_to_abuse_by_an_attachment_figure.

"Betrayal trauma theory suggests that psychogenic amnesia is an adaptive response to childhood abuse. When a parent or other powerful figure violates a fundamental ethic of human relationships, victims may need to remain unaware of the trauma not to reduce suffering but rather to promote survival. Amnesia enables the child to maintain an attachment with a figure vital to survival, development, and thriving. Analysis of developmental needs suggests that the degree to which the most fundamental human ethics are violated can influence the nature, form, and processes of trauma and responses to trauma."

4. Champe, Diane. "Effects of Maltreatment on Brain Development." *About EDCI*, www.edcinstitute.org/library/120-effects-and-impact/106-effects-of-maltreatment-on-brain-development.html

Effects of Maltreatment on Brain Development

Scientists are beginning to see the evidence of altered brain functioning as a result of early abuse and neglect. Growth in each region of a baby's brain largely depends on receiving stimulation which spurs activity in that region. This stimulation forms the foundation for learning. For additional information please refer to:

"Understanding the Effects of Maltreatment on Early Brain Development," National Clearinghouse on Child Abuse and Neglect Information (HHS), 2001.

Researchers use the term plasticity to describe the way the brain creates, strengthens, and discards synapses and neuronal pathways in response to the environment. The brain's plasticity is the reason that environment plays a vital role in brain development.

The ability to adapt to our environment is a part of normal development. All children need stimulation and nurturance for healthy development. If these are lacking – if a child's caretakers are indifferent or hostile – the child's brain development may be impaired. Because the brain adapts to its environment, it will adapt to a negative environment just as readily as it will adapt to a positive environment.

The effects of abuse and neglect on the developing brain during children's first few years can result in various mental health problems. For example:

- Diminished growth in the left hemisphere may increase the risk for depression.

- Irritability in the limbic system can set the stage for the emergence of panic disorder and posttraumatic stress disorder (PTSD).
- Smaller growth in the hippocampus and limbic abnormalities can increase the risk of dissociative disorders and memory impairments.
- Impairment in the connection between the two brain hemispheres has been linked to symptoms of attention-deficit/hyperactivity disorder (ADHD).
- Severely neglected children who have been deprived of sensory stimulation – including touch, movement, and sound – may be at risk for Sensory Integration Disorder
- Children who have been raised in environments that totally disregarded their needs for comfort, stimulation, and affection may be at risk for attachment disorders.

This research continues to demonstrate the serious, long-term consequences of abuse and neglect on brain development, and subsequent physical, cognitive, emotional, and social growth.

5. Champe, Diane. "Long Term Effects of Abuse." *About EDCI*, www.edcinstitute.org/library/120-effects-and-impact/108-long-term-effects.html

Long Term Effects of Abuse

If a survivor of child sexual abuse has not been in therapy or been helped along the way to cope with his/her abuse history, there is a range of effects that stem from the abuse. Depending upon each individual survivor's trauma history, the following list provides the common effects many survivors must deal with as a result of their abuse:

- Anxiety
- Post-Traumatic Stress Disorder (PTSD)
- Complex PTSD due to prolonged trauma
- Dissociation
- Depression
- Eating Disorders
- Impaired "self" and other boundaries
- Interpersonal and relational difficulties
- Parenting difficulties
- Memory impairment
- Personality Disorders
- Re-victimization
- Self-blame
- Sexual difficulties
- Substance use/abuse

6. Faupel, Susan. "Chapter 2: Etiology of Adult Sexual Offending by Susan Faupel, M.S.W., and Roger Przybylski." *Chapter 2: Etiology of Adult Sexual Offending | Sex Offender Management Assessment and Planning Initiative*, smart.gov/SOMAPI/sec1/ch2_etiology.html

The juvenile offender can be characterized as the following:

- Uses another child as a sexual outlet
- Does not consider the other's feelings
- Typically pre-plans and watches for opportunities to abuse
- Engages in a repetitious pattern of behavior
- Maintains secrecy through bribery, threats, and coercion
- May be motivated by revenge

7. "Dissociative Disorders." *Mayo Clinic*, Mayo Foundation

for Medical Education and Research, 17 Nov. 2017, www.mayoclinic.org/diseases-conditions/dissociative-disorders/symptoms-causes/syc-20355215

Dissociative disorders are mental disorders that involve experiencing a disconnection and lack of continuity between thoughts, memories, surroundings, actions and identity. People with dissociative disorders escape reality in ways that are involuntary and unhealthy and cause problems with functioning in everyday life.

Symptoms depend on the type of dissociative disorders you have, but may include:

- Memory loss (amnesia) of certain time periods, events, people and personal information
- A sense of being detached from yourself and your emotions
- A perception of the people and things around you as distorted and unreal
- A blurred sense of identity
- Significant stress or problems in your relationships, work or other important areas of your life
- Inability to cope well with emotional or professional stress
- Mental health problems, such as depression, anxiety, and suicidal thoughts and behaviors

8. Hartney, Elizabeth. "10 Reasons the Cycle of Sexual Abuse Continues." *Verywell Mind*, Verywell Mind, 4 May 2019, www.verywellmind.com/the-cycle-of-sexual-abuse-22460
"If the connection between abuse and "love" is made

early in life, the feelings of shame and anger, which naturally happen as a consequence of the abuse, can become mixed up with sexual feelings, leading to confusion in the person who experienced the abuse. These feelings may become interpreted as feelings of love and passion. People who have been abused may not realize other, healthier, ways of feeling in relationships that are possible."

"They believe they are attracted to or feeling love for their abuser, sometimes even thinking they have a special connection to the abuser, as it taps into feelings of intimacy associated with the abuse, that were imprinted at a very early age. So when they are later abused in an intimate relationship, they perceive the familiar feelings of shame and anger as love and passion."

"When emotional abuse is severe and ongoing, a victim may lose their entire sense of self, sometimes without a single mark or bruise. Instead, the wounds are invisible to others, hidden in the self-doubt, worthlessness and self-loathing the victim feels. "Consequences of emotional abuse are just as severe as those from physical abuse. They can no longer see themselves realistically and will never be good enough for anyone else."

"Emotional abuse can cause a number of health problems including everything from depression and anxiety to stomach ulcers, eating disorders, and insomnia."

9. Research has found that abuse by those who are female is more emotionally damaging than abuse committed by males.

One of the long-term effects by a male child who is abused by a female is intense rage towards women, low-esteem, and a need to always be in control which creates difficulties in relationships with women.

10a. Profile of an Abuser

1. Jealousy: questioning partner constantly about whereabouts, jealous of the time she or he spends away from him or her
2. Controlling behavior; the victim cannot get a job, leave the house.
3. Isolation; makes partner move away from family and friends so that she depends on him or her solely for support
4. Holds very rigid gender roles; partner's job is to cater to the abuser

Men who abuse are clever, smart, and extremely charming. Most of these men have a personality that draws people in, he is adept at charming, deceiving and manipulating. Most batterers are seen as Jekyll and Hyde because of the stark contrast in their public and private selves.

10b. The Abuse Cycle

- **Build-Up Phase** - The tension builds.
- **Stand-Over Phase** - Verbal attacks increase.
- **Explosion Phase** - A violent outburst occurs.
- **Remorse Phase** - You shouldn't have pushed me, it was your fault!
- **Pursuit Phase** - It will never happen again, I promise.
- **Honeymoon Phase** - See, we don't have any problems!

While this cycle is typical of domestic violence that is physical, other forms of domestic abuse that often accompany the physical violence as a means to further control include verbal abuse, psychological abuse, and emotional abuse.

11. Anonymous. "Don't Ignore Incest: Advice from an Incest Survivor." *KevinMD.com*, KevinMD.com, 16 Oct. 2018, www.kevinmd.com/blog/2018/10/dont-ignore-incest-advice-from-an-incest-survivor.html

ADDITIONAL RESOURCES FOR SHATTERING THE TABOO

Great Valley Publishing Company, Inc. *Sibling Sexual Abuse - Uncovering the Secret,*
   www.socialworktoday.com/archive/111312p18.shtml

"The very nature of sibling incest is so abhorrent to much of the public, and to many professionals who could play a significant role in realizing the goal of helping victims and survivors, that they don't want to believe it exists. By incorporating heightened awareness of sibling incest with proactive approaches to intervention, social workers can begin to combat this hidden social problem. Victims can be helped to disclose their secrets earlier, leading to better treatment outcomes, and survivors can be helped to resolve mental health and behavioral problems. Social workers can be instrumental in uncovering sibling incest on both societal and individual levels. As historical advocates for populations with problems that society ignores, social workers can be the leaders for the hidden population affected by sibling sexual abuse."

REPORT CHILD ABUSE — IT'S THE LAW

"Child Abuse." *Mayo Clinic*, Mayo Foundation for Medical Education and Research, 5 Oct. 2018, www.mayoclinic.org/diseases-conditions/child-abuse/symptoms-causes/syc-20370864

If you have reasons to believe a child may be a victim of physical, sexual, emotional abuse, or neglect, you are required by law to report it immediately to the local child protective service office or law enforcement.

ACKNOWLEDGMENTS

To my Cherished Children: Thank you for understanding my need to write this book. For all the times I had to call you back because I was still writing. For the times you caught me when I was pretending to listen, when my mind was preoccupied. Thank you for turning out to be the awesome adults I knew you would be. I treasure your ability to love and be there for each other. I will always love all of you; you will always be my world. Always!

To Bre: Thank you for standing by my son through it all, and for loving him unconditionally. And, of course, my endless thanks for my beautiful grandson.

To Jen: Thank you for my awesome grandsons.

To Karen: Thank you for taking such good care of my children when I needed time to get my shit together and for being such a good and loyal friend.

To Jesse: For loving my princess and for putting up with everything that makes her royal. Ask her to marry you and get it over with; I promise she'll say yes.

To my Darling Husband: Your love and support, all the endless hours, all the frozen pizzas you had to toss in the oven for dinner. For my constant reply, "the book will be done soon!" Holding me through all of my many nightmares, and for helping me sort out all the baggage I brought into our marriage. For always understanding my codependence when it comes to our kids. I'm still working on it, Hercules. Here's to the next chapter in our lives.

To Wendy Lou, Bird, Patty, and Kerri: For the endless questions I had about our family's past, I know some of it wasn't pleasant. For supporting and encouraging me to keep going. And, most of all, for always walking alongside me so I wasn't ever walking this road alone. I couldn't have survived without all of you.

To Sonny: For pulling me out of my shell and for helping me to shoot for the stars. You kept at me, making me dig deeper than I had ever done before. You put words to my feelings in a way that conveyed what I meant to say. Together, we got to the most honest portrayal of my experiences. You're now in my circle and know me better than I know myself.

To Bre, Jen, Liv, Marilyn, and Taylor: For all your hours of beta-reading and proofreading. Your suggestions and ideas were priceless.

To my Grandchildren Nicholas, Dawson, and Brayden: Thank you for exceeding all of my expectations. For our many fun times at grandma and grandpa's house. Remember when Mom and Dad leave, only Namma's rules apply.

ABOUT THE AUTHOR

Newcomer author and advocate Michelle Barry sheds light on the shroud of secrecy which often accompanies the shame of incest. She continues to educate herself and others on fearless survivorship. Her goal is to create a network of advocates who work with incest survivors nationwide. She wants to help survivors navigate through the sensitive period following disclosure of their abuse to family and friends. Support is unpredictable and the impact on family dynamics are significant. Often the best support comes from another survivor. She resides in Minnesota with her supportive husband, her five adult children, and her three, irresistible, grandchildren who live nearby. Her devotion to her family ensures that every branch of her family tree is nurtured by unwavering love for many generations to come.

To contact Michelle, visit www.michelle-barry-author.com

Contact the Author through her social media at:

Facebook:
facebook.com/michellebarryauthor/
Twitter:
twitter.com/MBarryAuthor
Instagram:
instagram.com/michellebarryauthor/

MICHELLE'S DAD WORKING IN THE COPPER MINES, 1954

MICHELLE'S DAD, DRINKING BEER WITH RUSTY, 1955

MICHELLE'S MOM ON HER WEDDING DAY

MOM, DYLAN, CAITLYN, QUINT AND DAMIAN

CAITLYN, 2 YEARS OLD

DYLAN, 2ND GRADE AND QUINT

THE FARM

QUINT, 17

PATTY AND DYLAN / MICHELLE, MOM, AND QUINT

MICHELLE, WENDY LOU, ROGER AT BIRTHDAY PARTY

MICHELLE, DAMIAN, TWINS AND COUSIN BETTY

K-8TH GRADE SCHOOL STUDENTS

MICHELLE AND MOM, 1977

MICHELLE AND MOM, 1986

DAD AND MOM

ROGER, 10 YEARS OLD

MICHELLE, 6 YEARS OLD

ROGER, 18 YEARS OLD / MICHELLE, 16 YEARS OLD

Michelle and Dad getting firewood

Dad at his homestead

Michelle and Dad with his childhood tree

Dad and Aunt Jesse

MICHELLE ON WEDDING DAY TO JACK

WENDY LOU GETTING MICHELLE READY FOR WEDDING DAY

CAITLYN, DAD, AND MICHELLE

KYRA, PATTY, CAITLYN, AMBER, WENDY LOU, AND
MICHELLE

WENDY LOU AND JOEY

MICHELLE AND JOEY

JOEY, 1 YEAR OLD

CPSIA information can be obtained
at www.ICGtesting.com
Printed in the USA
BVHW041739250620
582335BV00011B/201